SURPRISING
LIGHT

Stories of Love, Mercy, and Grace

David G. Bowen

WESTBOW
PRESS®
A DIVISION OF THOMAS NELSON
& ZONDERVAN

WestBow Press books may be ordered through booksellers or by contacting:

WestBow Press
A Division of Thomas Nelson & Zondervan
1663 Liberty Drive
Bloomington, IN 47403
www.westbowpress.com
844-714-3454

ISBN: 978-1-6642-8994-9 (sc)
ISBN: 978-1-6642-8995-6 (hc)
ISBN: 978-1-6642-8993-2 (e)

Library of Congress Control Number: 2023901113

Print information available on the last page.

WestBow Press rev. date: 01/26/2023

This book is dedicated to my Aunt Pauline Norton, to my Mother Carolyn Bowen and to my daughter Lesley Ayn Bowen. Your memory grows brighter with every day!

CONTENTS

Chapter 1   Amy's Gift...1

Chapter 2   Presenting! 5

Chapter 3   Up! 10

Chapter 4   Deep Shadows..13

Chapter 5   Indeed!... 17

Chapter 6   Can Hope Be a Seed?.................................21

Chapter 7   Pure Joy 25

Chapter 8   Her Mom..30

Chapter 9   The Pew on the Back Row 35

Chapter 10   Whatcha Gonna Do?.................................38

Chapter 11   The Timing of God 42

Chapter 12   Letters After Your Name...........................45

Chapter 13   Thanks for the Years 49

Chapter 14   Let the Children Come 51

Chapter 15   Just When We Need It...............................55

Chapter 16   Just Like a Good Neighbor.........................58

Chapter 17   They Were in Awe! 61

Chapter 18   What a Fellowship, What a Joy Divine! 66

Chapter 19   My Mother Made a Delicious English
Trifle 70

Chapter 20   Our Friend Ruthie Geva Has Died..........73

Chapter 21   Germs in the Communion Cup.................76

Chapter 22   Leaving on a Jet Plane … 79

Chapter 23   Reminders That We Are Not in Charge...84

Chapter 24   One Sunday in Lithonia 88

Chapter 25   Getting Ready to Disciple......................92

Chapter 26   One Evening Near Ansley Mall 95

Chapter 27   It's All Downhill from Helen, Georgia......99

Chapter 28   Please Describe an Instructor for Me 104

Chapter 29   My First Sunday … and Theirs 108

Chapter 30   Words to Show My Heart 112

Chapter 31   The Friday Before That First Sunday 115

Chapter 32   Gnawing Locusts! 119

Chapter 33   Eyes to See..125

Chapter 34   Macon in August! 127

Chapter 35   What Can You Do? 131

Chapter 36   Light As A Feather 134

Chapter 37   A Friend for Life 140

Chapter 38   Connecting the Dogs............................ 145

Chapter 39   The Newbie Is Always Sent! 148

Chapter 40   Won't Ya Let Me Take You on a Sea
             Cruise! 153

Chapter 41   I-75 … Far From Civilization 157

Chapter 42   It Would Have Been Enough! 160

Chapter 43   It Was on TV 163

Chapter 44   John 167

1

AMY'S GIFT

> "You have turned for me my mourning into dancing; you have loosed my sackcloth and clothed me with gladness, that my glory may sing your praise and not be silent. O LORD my God, I will give thanks to you forever!"
>
> —*Psalm 30:11–12 (ESV)*

WHEN OUR DAUGHTER, LESLEY AYN, DIED IN 1995, MY sister, Judy, my nieces, Amy, Jennifer, and Laura, and nephew, Brian, were out of the country with their husband and father, Col. John Mandeville, of the United States Army. They were unable to attend Lesley's funeral.

Over the ensuing years, my sermons about Lesley's place in my life, articles concerning her death and funeral, information about the cabin at Camp Glisson, my doctoral work, and all kinds of other things done to remember Lesley have been sent to Judy's family.

I never knew that my niece Amy has been keeping copies of all these memorials and has quietly pondered them in her heart. She used them to frame her mirror at home and then again during the years she spent at college.

I did not know how much Amy loved Lesley or how much she missed her cousin. I did not know that Amy is also a poet and has written her grief over Lesley's death and the death of my father, Bill Bowen, her gramps.

Part of my grief, especially in the first few years after Lesley's death, was the pain from being asked to perform weddings for young women I had known and loved all their lives. The pain was in knowing that I would never walk my daughter down an aisle for her own wedding. Unless you understand that, you might misunderstand part of my heart. All of this is to tell you how mixed and confused some of my feelings were two weeks ago, when my wife, Billie, and I traveled to Virginia, near Charlottesville, for my niece Jennifer's wedding. I put on my preacher face and made sure I did not feel much hurt as this lovely young woman married her fiancé, Chris. My niece Amy was Jennifer's maid of honor. All three of Judy's daughters are elegantly tall and drop-dead gorgeous, and Amy has brunette hair and big feet—just like her cousin Lesley Ayn.

I did OK with all the prewedding stuff, and I did OK with the rehearsal and the rehearsal dinner. I even did well with the wedding itself. It was set on a mountaintop that felt straight out of *The Sound of Music*. However, we had a string quartet instead of Julie Andrews. I must be honest and tell you that I did have some quiet tears, but they were as much for the joy of love and celebration of family as they were for me.

The reception following the wedding was wonderful.

After the bluegrass band entertained us during a light barbeque by the lake, we moved inside a lodge for a delightful meal. You're probably not surprised that I was asked to offer the blessing before we ate. After dinner, a dance floor was cleared, and the DJ from Miami, Florida, played lots of good old sixties and seventies music like all decent human beings love. I was blessed to be with so much of my family. Billie and I were even able to dance together.

There was a quiet moment, and then I heard the words, "It's time for the father-daughter dance, so girls, find your dads and take the floor."

My heart shattered. I was partly stunned at being stunned. I sat numbly while all the fathers and daughters began to slow-dance in lovely pairs. With great pride and affection, I saw the bride, Jennifer, dancing with her father. I saw her sister Laura with my nephew, Brian. However, I did not see my niece Amy move around the edge of the lodge, back in the shadows, where the light did not reveal her presence—until she touched my arm and said with tears in her eyes, "Uncle David, may I have this dance in honor of Lesley?"

I could not speak. There were no words. I stood and took this elegant young woman in my arms to dance.

Then it happened.

Like in the dance scene in the film *Ghosts*, when Whoopi Goldberg becomes the dead man for the grieving widow, my niece Amy, by the grace of God, became Lesley in that moment. And I got to dance with my daughter at a wedding. In the hour that passed after the song ended, Amy revealed to Billie and me all the stories of the past years

2
PRESENTING!

"The waters of baptism do that for you, not by washing away dirt from your skin but by presenting you through Jesus's resurrection before God with a clear conscience."

—*1 Peter 3:21 (MSG)*

HER NAME IS DARLENE.

She ended up in the foster care program of Henry County, Georgia. It was not her fault; she never did anything wrong. But she went from foster home to foster home until she finally settled in a good home outside McDonough, Georgia, on Turner Church Road.

I had just been appointed as the pastor to the congregation of the Turner Methodist Church. That congregation met in a white clapboard building perched on carefully built stacks of river rocks that formed its foundation. The building had been constructed in 1821 on what then had been the massive Turner plantation. It had survived the Civil War, during which it had been used as a horse stable for cavalry officers in General Sherman's army. Leaving the church building, you would travel up a long driveway to Turner Church Road. From there, you could either turn right and head back to McDonough or turn left and head over toward the real country. Straight ahead was a pond, about an acre wide, right at the road. The pond belonged to Mary Lou. People called it a fishpond, but it was mainly used to water cows.

All this geography brings me to Darlene's decision to be baptized. I met with her, and we made a list of what she wanted. She understood that, as her pastor, I was to baptize her. What a joy! Now I was going to celebrate the profession of faith and the baptism of a young believer in Jesus Christ.

Darlene asked to be fully immersed in water. Our book of worship covers immersion as an acceptable choice to be used in celebrating a baptism. I owned a copy of this text and had read some of it. She wanted her baptism to be on a Sunday after morning worship at the Turners' church. The congregation had very few young adults or children, so this would be a wonderful day for them.

Darlene asked her brother to film the service because he said that no Methodist had "rightly" baptized anyone in Henry County as long as anybody could remember. She selected Mary Lou's pond as the location for her baptism. Again, this was a cow pond that came with all the accompanying gifts that cattle share in such a watering hole.

I'd had an ingrown toenail on my left big toe for many years longer than I should have, and I had "seminaried" through the pain. My suffering had finally reached the point that, a month earlier, I found a podiatrist and got it surgically removed. My foot was heavily bandaged, and I had cut the toe section out of my Sunday preaching shoes so I could walk without enormous pain. But when Darlene asked me to baptize her, what was I to say? You have already figured that I said yes.

Darlene and I were satisfied that we had covered her list. We were ready to announce her baptism to the congregation. However, we had not planned for the freezing temperatures caused when an Arctic clipper met moisture from the Gulf of Mexico. Fortunately, the Sunday morning of Darlene's baptism had warmed to above fifty degrees. And even better, most of the ice around the edge of Mary Lou's pond had begun to melt. But best of all, the cows had been moved beyond a barbed-wire fence that ran around the baptismal site.

Despite the checklist, I was still left with a wounded but rapidly healing toe. I knew enough about thick plastic and duct tape to fashion a waterproof enclosure for my toe. I designed a sleeve out of 6-mil black sheeting. The thing would run from the sole of my left foot almost up to my waist. I would secure it with hundreds of yards of silver duct tape. I did not have enough time to do a test run using my protective device, but I was a Methodist pastor with one wedding and one funeral under my belt. What could possibly be the problem? (It turned out to be the wondrous buoyancy of things when sealed and shoved under water to a depth of about a human waist.)

Sunday dawned. We worshipped in the sanctuary as

the morning warmed just a bit. Most of the congregation accompanied Darlene and her photographer brother up the driveway and to a collection point at the edge of the pond. I rushed to the church's restroom to begin the process of sheathing myself in thick plastic and tape. The left leg of my suit pants now fit in such a way that I was channeling Chester on *Gunsmoke* as I made my way to join the crowd that was anxiously awaiting my arrival.

The cows, alerted to human movement, suspected that hay or some other edible might be forthcoming if they just mooed loudly and frequently enough. They were fully cooperative. The moo-cow choir also accompanied Darlene as she repeated those ancient words of faith in Jesus that were once silently acknowledged but now publicly declared.

I took her hand, and together, we stepped into the ankle-deep "mud" of the pond bottom. We walked deeper into the water even though I left both of my Sunday shoes somewhere buried somewhere and never retrieved them.

Math had never been my strong suit. But now I was wishing I had paid more attention to things like how to calculate the lift produced by a contained volume of air relative to an increasing depth of water.

My left foot and leg were attempting to float all around me.

Thank goodness Darlene and I had reached the desired depth in the pond, also a depth where the water was the cleanest. I was balancing on one foot.

Above all things, I was fighting to remain as "pastoral" as possible for the film, whose director/photographer was now yelling helpful instructions so I would face in the right direction for "maximum Channel 2 WSB-TV coverage."

I invited Darlene to take a deep breath and to hold that breath and her nose as I immersed her under the water in the name of the Father and of the Son and of the Holy Spirit.

She did just that. As she stood and shook some of the water from her hair and face, the congregation began to cheer and applaud.

I know that the lives of two fragile humans were forever changed in that moment. Can you imagine water could do that?

3
UP!

"I know a man in Christ who, fourteen years ago, was caught up to the third heaven— whether in the body or out of the body I do not know; God knows. And I know that this man was caught up into Paradise—whether in the body or out of the body I do not know, God knows—and he heard things that cannot be told, which man may not utter."

2 Corinthians 12:2–4 (RSV)

IT WAS A SPRING ATLANTA DAY. THE BRIGHTNESS MANDATED sunglasses, and the pollen asked for eye drops. I was at Emory University Hospital to donate blood platelets for a leukemia patient who was to remain anonymous.

The donation procedure is beyond my ability or capability to explain. Basically, the nurse draws blood out of one arm and tubes it into an Aphaeresis machine. The machine then draws off the highly prized blood platelets, and then the remainder of the blood is placed back into the donor's other arm through a different tube. This machine costs about what we would pay for our new car plus "disposables," which run several thousand dollars per patient.

This type of donating had been my privilege for several years. My ancestral DNA had arranged for me to be blood type O-negative, and the demand is great. Besides, when I donate, I get warm blankets all round me. I also get microwave-heated saline bags on really good body parts. Then I get all the orange juice and Nutter Butter cookies I want before I go home.

Oh, did I mention you also got to watch your choice of a current film while you donate?

On this particular donation day, I was having a really good day. The nurse who took care of me made sure I was comfy. When the selected number of platelets had been collected, I sat with juice and cookies for a while to make sure I was not going to faint, fall over, or suffer from anything requiring emergency medical attention.

As I prepared to leave, my nurse said, "The leukemia patient for whom you have given platelets today has given permission to visit. She wants to thank you in person. Would you like to do that?"

I was, at first, somewhere between embarrassed and bewildered. This was the first time in all my donating that the person receiving my blood had asked me to visit.

I said, "Yes, I would be honored."

My heart did a slight fluttering thing as I was led down several corridors and hallways to a private hospital room. The patient was lying in her bed with a few family members gathered around.

We spoke those gracious words of "thank you" and "you are most welcome." I admit that I wanted to shed a tear or two in that room, but I was able to keep it together.

I left and made my way to the hospital parking deck to find my car. As I started the engine, I remembered that I had a brand-new CD still unwrapped in the box. It was *Go West Young Man* by Michael W. Smith. I opened the disc, popped it into the player, and arbitrarily decided to play selection number nine. The piece had a Latin title, "Agnus Dei," and featured the voices of the American Boy Choir with Nathan Wadley as soloist.

Have you heard that piece? I had not. Fortunately, as Nathan's haunting voice began the song's melodic chant, I was able to pull the car over to the side of the road that wound out of the parking deck and onto a side street.

Suddenly, there was a burst of dazzling light that filled the car. I was not able to breathe for a moment or two. Then the windows and doors of my car seemed to blow away. I was left with nothing but the voices of Michael W. Smith and this boys' choir pouring through my ears and into my heart. It was then that the flood of tears began.

As I type this, I am playing that CD again and weeping to the sound of "Worthy is the Lamb."

It is once again a bright spring afternoon. Sometimes that which we may not utter in words can be sung. The Lord Almighty reigns!

4

DEEP SHADOWS

"The people who walked in darkness have seen a great light. For those who lived in a land of deep shadows—light! sunbursts of light!"

—*Isaiah 9:2 (The Message)*

UNTIL OUR DAUGHTER, LESLEY AYN, DIED, THE HARDEST I had ever been hit was in the late autumn of my senior year in high school. We played Elbert County in the "Granite Bowl" for the right to advance in the Georgia State football playoffs. The hits to which I refer are what you suffer from as you go across the middle of the field on a pass play, and you catch the ball. However, you also catch the shoulders and the helmet of a defensive back who has been waiting his whole high school career for such a game as this.

The hits were clean, but the pain was not. Human ribs are constructed like a flexible network to surround the lungs and heart so that damage happens to the rib cage and not these vital organs. When those bones are cracked, your breath pauses. Your nervous system is stunned. Your insides ache just as your outsides are going to about an hour later.

Although we played hard, we didn't win. I remember withdrawing into the adolescent quiet of a game lost. Nothing can be said to ease all the places that hurt after such a loss.

I learned of Lesley's death on a Saturday morning in September, just as the football season was really getting under way. I remember seeing the faces of my wife and several friends who were crossing the lawn of a retreat center to tell me the tragic news. When I saw them coming toward me, I knew it was bad news. I then realized it was about one of our children. I am told that I cried out, "It's Lesley," as I slumped to the floor.

I had been awakened after being unable to breathe or see or hear for a time earlier that morning. The EMT logs and witness testimonies revealed that she had died at the time of my "fugue state."

When a person dies, there are plans that must be made. One is called a visitation, which is usually held the night before the funeral service. Another is the funeral itself. Will there be music? Who will speak? Where will she be buried?

A celebration of Lesley's life was held on a rather dreary day, weather that I thought was entirely appropriate. I do remember that our friend Donna played and sang "Sanctuary," which was one of Les's favorites. She had learned the song while attending a week of worship and activities at Camp Glisson in North Georgia. I also recall that my friends Wayne and Rex stood on either side of me to hold me up as I told the story of an Easter-season reconciliation between my daughter and myself.

I thank all of you who reached out to me and my family during that time.

Psychiatrist and writer Elizabeth Kübler-Ross outlines the stages of grief and has alerted the world to how powerful the onset and the duration of shock can be. For me, my shock was pale ashen and enduring gray. That color is said to be somewhere between white and black and is therefore a neutral color or an achromatic color. Until that time, most of my life had ranged from deep pastels to a vibrant loud box of the best Crayola colors. But after my daughter's death, everything and everyone moved in slow motion and without emotion.

Oh, I cried when I could. But I felt like a 2-RPM record in a 78-RPM world. It is recorded in the minutes of 1995 that I met people, preached sermons, taught classes, and generally acted sort of like myself. That is what I offered to the world around me. Inside, I was not sure about life itself.

Several months passed, and my friend David called me. He and his wife had two extra tickets to a concert by Lawrence Chewning at a local church house. He wondered if Billie and I would join them. Every fiber of my being strained and stretched with how to gracefully bow out of this invitation just as I had done with most everything public to this date. But after a season of struggle to say no to David, my mouth opened and I said, "Yes, we would like to join you."

I started to bolt like a frightened deer when I saw that our seats were in the middle of the third row. Worse,

Lawrence had arranged his microphone, chair, and guitar right at the front edge of the platform. We were almost going to be sitting with him as he sang.

You have probably already guessed that my worst fear would be the song that he would, of course, choose to open his time with us.

The time for the concert to begin was upon us. Lawrence walked to his mike and simply began to play a song that I had never heard. He sang:

> I have journeyed through the long dark night
> Out on the open sea, by faith alone
> Sight unknown; and yet His eyes were watching me.
> The anchor holds
> Though the ship is battered
> The anchor holds
> Though the sails are torn
> I have fallen on my knees as I face the raging seas
> The anchor holds in spite of the storm.

I believe that if you look carefully at the edge of a storm, you can see the faintest hint of a light that has not yet come. Praise God, it is so!

5

INDEED!

"Indeed, there are those who are last who will
be first, and first who will be last."

—*Luke 13:30 (NIV)*

Do you believe that dreams can come true? I was born
loving camp meetings. I had always dreamed and fantasized
that one day, I would preach at one of the evening services
at a camp meeting near you.

I did eventually get to a county fair. And to a baseball
game. And to an Okefenokee Swamp canoe trip. But for
all the early years of my ministry, I was never invited to a
camp meeting.

In the late 1970s, I moved to a wonderful congregation
in East Cobb County. The adult choir of that congregation
had prepared and had been presenting a work in worship
called *Celebrate Life* by Buryl Red and Ragan Courtney.

Like *Hair* way back in that day, this musical presentation
of the life of Jesus needs to be seen and heard. In fact, the
entire presentation can be viewed on YouTube. And so

it came to pass that I was privileged to join the cast and the choir of *Celebrate Life*. Just FYI, I was the character Matthew.

One day my long-awaited phone call came at the church office. The voice identified the person as a member of a well-known family in our community. The purpose of the call was to tell me that the camp meeting committee had contacted all the preachers they wanted to come and preach, but they had failed to secure a preacher for the Friday night evening worship that was just a few days away. Was I interested?

Lord, have mercy! Christ, have mercy! "Yes," I said.

"Good. We want to sign you up for that evening. There is one thing. You will need to pay $150.00 to be able to preach. We have expenses," they told me.

"No problem."

"One other thing. We do not have special music for that service. Do you have a choir at your church?"

"Yes. They are so good; I would love to have them share this service with me."

"OK. They will need to pay $150.00 to be able to sing. We have expenses."

I agreed, and we were signed on the dotted line for Friday night at seven o'clock.

That night came true. The choir and I arrived at the marvelous log tabernacle. The building was complete with a tin roof that allows rain to be properly heard at night—but not gale-force winds and rain falling at about three inches an hour like we had that night.

It was a good thing the crowd filled only half of the

tabernacle. That way, when the rain and wind entered the open side of the structure, the people could move in mass to the dry seats on the other side.

The choir and I were up on stage, so we didn't need to move—although we ducked when the fierce lightening ripped through the sky overhead.

When worship began, I was at peace with being the last person called. At least I had been called. Yet, I could not let the moment pass without opening my remarks and my sermon with a story.

Once, there was a small boy in a small town. The boy had a long, yellow pet dog. That dog accompanied the boy everywhere he went. On afternoon, the boy and his friend were passing a local tavern when a guy with too much under his snoot walked out with a pit bull on a chain.

The man challenged the boy and set his enormous bulldog on the pair. The long yellow dog growled once, and the sound that came from the pit bull was of terror. The pit bull ran away as if it had been frightened nearly to death, though it was never touched. The man asked the boy just what kind of dog he had.

The boy grinned and said it had been an alligator until it lost its tail and he had painted it yellow.

OK, I was a lot more at peace after I told my story, so I moved on to my sermon. But the surprises for the evening were not finished.

While I was preaching, a car that was parked in one of the spaces at the back of the tabernacle had its emergency brakes fail. Once it was set free, the car rolled down a brief incline and came to rest with a resounding *THUNK* on one of the wooden pillars that supported the roof of the structure under which we were gathered.

Thankfully, the pillar held, and we collectively let out a sigh of relief.

The surprises were over, and my sermon was adequate for the occasion. I was blessed.

At the close of my preaching, I was transformed into Matthew and began to loudly say, "He is alive!"

On cue, members of the choir began to repeat the phrase louder and louder until some thirty of us were nearly shouting with joy. And so, at last, the camp meeting congregation did what countless generations of Jesus lovers have done: we sang praises!

6

CAN HOPE BE A SEED?

"And some seed fell on rich soil and produced fruit."

—*Mark 4:8 (New American Bible, revised edition)*

DID YOU KNOW OUR MOTHER? HER NAME IS CAROLYN Judith Norton Bowen. We lost her to death, but she remains one of the greatest characters ever to grace this earth. She was a prototype of a "blessed mess."

When our father died, Mom asked, "For as long as I am alive, can I stay in my own home?" It was not really a question. I understood that.

The answer was, "Yes."

Some five years later, it became obvious that she would no longer be able to stay at home, even with twenty-four-hour sitter and nurse care.

It hurts, doesn't it?

She agreed to enter the Providence Healthcare Facility

in Thomaston, Georgia. However, she refused to do anything but lie in bed and attempt to die.

I made visits as often as I could. The song she sang had two verses: "Why am I still alive?" and "I want to go home." Nothing helped, not antidepression meds or physical this or healthy that.

She just laid in bed and grieved. Some of you know, don't you?

Then one day, I drove to Thomaston for a visit. When I entered her room, there against the bed was her walker, but with no Carolyn holding onto it.

There was also her wheelchair, empty, with no Carolyn in it.

The bed was neatly made, but there was no Mom.

I went to the worst-case scenario in my mind. You do understand, don't you? She had died. My mother was dead, and …

You, see when my father died, I was not called until later that night. I could not be there with him. I still hurt about that sometimes.

You do understand, don't you?

I rushed to the nursing station to find out what had happened. They said, "Your mother is in the beauty parlor getting her hair cut." Now I had to wait about an hour and a half!

Carolyn Norton Bowen of Athens, Georgia, had not allowed her hair to be cut in more than fifty years. That's *fifty* years!

I knew it. They were telling me this story because Martians had come and taken my mother away and left some strange, short-haired woman in her place. Martians will do that, won't they?

I rushed to the beauty parlor, but she was not there. The attendant said, "Your mother had all her hair cut off and donated it to make a wig for a cancer patient. Now she has gone to have her nails done."

They could not be telling me the truth. My mother did not have her nails done. Mom did her own nails. Martians again.

I made my way to the nail salon, but she was not there, either. The attendant said, "She is in physical therapy doing her exercises." So I made my way to the physical therapy section.

Sure enough, there was a short-haired, lacquer-nailed, sharp-dressed, nondepressed woman who looked vaguely familiar to me sitting on an exercise bench, doing some arm lifts to music.

I sat down beside her. "What have the Martians done with my real mother?" I asked.

She laughed and said, "Oh, David. Wait until I am finished working out, and then you can join me and two friends for lunch. We are going off campus to the Peachtree Cafe for fried chicken."

I said, "Fine, Mom, but how will you get back to your room?"

Grinning, she said, "I will hold onto your arm and walk."

We got back to her room and, while we waited for her the friends to come, she said, "Do you know what?"

By this time, I did not know any what whatsoever.

I said, "No."

"There are women who don't want to be here."

I said, "No way."

She said, "Yes. These women come here depressed and angry."

"Imagine that."

"The manager has asked me to visit with women like that and encourage them not to be depressed and angry. That is now my purpose."

I stammered, "Do tell."

"Shall we go to lunch?"

It was the very best *yes* I had ever said.

7

PURE JOY

"Consider it pure joy, my brothers and sisters,
whenever you face trials of many kinds …"

—*James 1:2 (NIV)*

I LOVED MY CRYSTAL RADIO SET THAT I MADE IN AN EMPTY
cigar box. During the day, I could listen to any radio station
within five miles. But come nightfall, stations from as far
away as Chicago and New Orleans were all mine.

Then technology blew up all over the planet. In our
town, Mr. Massey got a TV with a screen larger than a
cubic squirrel. Sunday nights were *Bonanza* with phrases
like, "Be very careful falling in love with Hoss because bad
things would happen."

Even better than watching westerns were Wednesdays
watching the *Mickey Mouse Club*. Wednesdays were
"anything can happen day." Who could forget those zany
happenings with Jimmy and Annette? Woohoo!

I waited years for any other program to come close to
all the strange happening of "anything" days. My dream

was finally fulfilled when I became an ordained clergy who would perform weddings.

All of us clergy members have at least one wedding that we shall remember and embellish around campfires and hearths forever. For me, one of my all-time favorites was centered on a strong and rich love between David and Stephanie. They were my close friends. And besides, the rehearsal dinner was to be a chow-down on ribs and other delights at a restaurant called Ray's on the River.

Speaking of the rehearsal ...

The matron of honor was almost consumed with her solo that she believed would set the tone for the wedding. I figured it would move the spotlight from the marriage taking place onto her instead, but I held my tongue. I was more concerned that she got the groom's ring into my hand at the appropriate time in the service.

The dress code for the Friday night rehearsal was jeans and whatever comfort clothes the wedding party wanted to wear. Stephanie's dad was a full-grown adult. He easily could have played as a pulling guard for any team in the SEC. His job was to walk his daughter down the center aisle of the sanctuary, move her hand from his own arm to that of the groom, and then be seated beside his wife on the second row to my right.

The bride rehearsed in her jeans and boots, all the while forgetting that her cathedral-length and -width wedding dress was fifteen times the size of the space her father planned to occupy the next evening.

The food at Riverside was most excellent. The laughter

was deep, and we stayed far too long. But eventually, everyone made his or her way home.

The next day, we were presented with a beautiful Saturday evening. The sanctuary was filled with family and friends of the couple. Photographers were well represented. I checked in with Stephanie and David to make sure they had sufficient pregame butterflies. They did!

The hour arrived. The music began and so did the soloist for the evening. Each of the attendants made his or her way to join me at the altar. David and I waited for the music to change to announce that the bride and her father were coming to join us.

Stephanie's train would have filled any sanctuary. She was elegant and radiated her love for all who were gathered, especially for David. As planned, her father moved her hand from his own arm to that of the groom, and with a quarter turn, he took a giant step toward joining his wife.

Out of the corner of my eye, I saw him disappear to the floor. At the same time, I heard Stephanie's gown make all kinds of noises, as if someone had fallen into the train and was struggling either to stand up or crawl away.

Of course, it was her father who wrestled to save his life from dozens of yards of fabric. At last, he was able to crawl up the aisle and pop-up bedside his wife like a piece of embarrassed Pez candy. Stephanie managed to lean back far enough to avoid having her tumbling dad accidentally rip her dress off, and then she regained her posture and her composure.

The key to such a moment is to look at the mother of the bride. Her reaction to such happenings will give the officiant a guide as to how the rest of the wedding and the reception will go.

She was laughing and just patted her pop-up husband on his arm. Whew! The rest of the wedding was wonderful … until I asked the best man and the matron of honor for the rings. The best man cooperated and placed the ring in my hand. The matron whispered in an operatic voice, "No."

I whispered back, "Why not?"

She replied through her fast-clenching teeth, "Because I do not have it."

Matching her teeth, I asked, "Why not?"

She said, "Because I left it in your office."

I turned to Stephanie and told her that we had several choices about the ring. We could go ahead as if nothing had happened and not have the ring. We could ask one of the wedding party members to lend us a ring. Or we could pause and send a runner to my office for the ring. I also reminded her that it was her wedding, and it was her choice.

She wanted the ring that had been chosen for her wedding. I announced that I had mistakenly left a ring in my office and would one of the attendants go and retrieve it? Someone did. Everything after that went off without a hitch.

A few months later, we gathered at the home of the bride's parents to watch the video of the wedding. You could say it was a perfect evening.

We watched a "prima diva" have her moment. We watched a full-grown adult stumble over a magnificent dress, fall, crawl, and recover with great style. We watched a ring forgotten and a ring recovered. Most importantly, we witnessed a commitment made in love and the actions taken on that commitment.

There was little perfection in that ceremony, but oh, the joy that filled that room!

8
HER MOM

"Sir, we want to see Jesus. Can you help us?"
—*John 12:21 (The Message)*

FOR NINE YEARS, ELIZABETH AND HER FAMILY HAD ATTENDED the church I was serving. I had baptized their two children. I was privileged to work in vacation bible school and church plays with her husband and her. They were a hard-working, highly energetic, and very committed family in our congregation.

I knew about Elizabeth's mom from the prayer requests that had come to my attention over the years. Her mom had developed cancer later in her life. She had received all the treatments that were available, but nothing seemed to help with her disease. She and Elizabeth's dad even moved to Mexico so they would have access to some treatments that were not recognized as acceptable in the US.

Elizabeth's mom grew continually worse. She came to visit her daughter and family. Perhaps this would be the last opportunity to do so, and she especially wanted to have time with her grandchildren.

I had since moved from the area and was serving a new congregation in another county. The phone rang at my house. It was Elizabeth. She wanted to know if I would come and visit with her mom. I had the time, so I went.

During the drive, I was praying—eyes open, of course. I was asking God for the right words to say in such a delicate situation.

What were the right words?

Elizabeth's mom was much worse than I had anticipated. Her breathing was considerably slowed down. She had difficulty sitting up in a chair. She was physically exhausted, but she was deeply concerned.

Something was wrong. I asked her about it.

She said she had lived the very best life she knew how. She did not expect to receive any rewards for all that she had done through her church. Yet, there was something she wanted with all her heart before she died.

She wanted to see Jesus!

As she talked, I raced way ahead of her because I had convinced myself that the widely reported appearances of the Virgin Mary at a home near Conyers, Georgia, were the cause of her expressed desire to see Jesus.

Wrong!

I thank God that I decided to quit trying to know so much. I decided to include her in a conversation about her heart's desire. Elizabeth's mom had devoted her lifetime to lay ministries through the churches where she had worshipped. I was impressed by the incredible variety of ways that she had lived out her faith in Jesus Christ through being the very hands and feet of Him.

She began to glow with a deep energy as she described the meals-on-wheels recipients with whom she would visit and pray. She had made sure that anyone from her churches who was in the hospital or in a nursing home got personal care through calls and cards and visits.

She had even continued the vital lay ministries when she was physically suffering and under treatment for her cancer. Yet, with every story about these ministries, she would close by discounting what she had done, saying it was of no importance.

She was so insistent that her serving others in Jesus's name should be ignored.

Years ago, I had learned a lovely hymn during the time I spent in England with my children. The title is, "Sometimes a Light Surprises."

I knew that song was about God's Holy Spirit providing us with words or questions when we do not know what to ask or to say. In that moment with Elizabeth's mom, I silently prayed that some of God's surprising light would fall over me.

After her stories about her litany of her ministries and claiming that they were unimportant had run its course, I spoke.

"You cannot have it both ways. You cannot want to see Jesus with all your heart and at the same time discount what you have done for Him," I said.

I had her attention. I continued, "You have to choose. Do you want to see Jesus?"

"Yes," she said with great dignity.

I said, "Then you need to open your ears and your heart and hear what I am going to read."

I read Matthew 25:34–40 (The Message).

> Then the King will say to those on his right, "Enter, you who are blessed by my Father! Take what's coming to you in this kingdom. It's been ready for you since the world's foundation.
> And here's why:
> I was hungry and you fed me,
> I was thirsty and you gave me a drink,
> I was homeless and you gave me a room,
> I was shivering and you gave me clothes,
> I was sick and you stopped to visit,
> I was in prison and you came to me.'
>
> Then those "sheep" are going to say, "Master, what are you talking about? When did we ever see you hungry and feed you, thirsty and give you a drink? And when did we ever see you sick or in prison and come to you?' Then the King will say, "I'm telling the solemn truth: Whenever you did one of these things to someone overlooked or ignored, that was me—you did it to me."

I finished that scripture and waited. After a bit, Elizabeth's mom smiled deeply and said, "Oh my!"

I should not have been surprised at the burst of light around her.

9

THE PEW ON THE BACK ROW

"Make a joyful noise unto the LORD …"

—*Psalm 100:1 (KJV)*

DO YOU ALWAYS SIT IN THE SAME PLACE WHEN YOU ARE attending something in public? Like worship? John did. Always.

He sat in the last pew in the sanctuary every Sunday that he was in worship. From the pulpit I almost had to squint as I looked to my left to focus as far back as there were pews.

There was John. He was never my best friend, but we were friends. I respected him greatly. Mostly because of his work ethic. He raised cattle on his farm just outside of town. To feed them, he planted and cut and baled his own hay. Anyone who puts up hay deserves great respect. Amen?

Another thing I admired about John was his absolute clarity about music that could be sung in worship. We are a mess about "church music" today. Can I tell you how I have resolved this mess?

35

All music is "contemporary" on the day it is composed. All music is "traditional" on the day after it is composed. If we are playing or singing or offering music as part of our worship of God, then why all the ulcers, name-calling, and torn hair over which label you attach to the music?

Which brings us back to how John solved the worship-music issue.

He was raised to believe that there were only twelve hymns worthy of being sung in any sort of congregational gathering. That's right. Twelve hymns were all he would tolerate anytime and anywhere that hymns were offered.

How do you express displeasure when "your hymns" are not being selected and sung? John had this down pat. When the offending hymn was announced, he would glare at the pulpit area like he wished a torture of medieval proportions on the song leader or the pastor.

Then he would slam his hymnal shut with a vengeance that had been boiled to perfection over long years of suffering. Our hymnals were not the brown Cokesbury ones; neither were they the floppy-back blue ones. No, they were authentic and approved four-pounders with Psalms and services in the back.

Therefore, when John slammed his hymnal shut, he was able to call quite loud attention to his hymnic disapproval! All those years of hay-baling were put to good use as the pages of that hymnal were compressed in his massive hands.

But wait. There's more.

His final piece was to jam the now-slammed hymnal back into the hymnal rack on the back of his pew. John used the same energy that had slung decades of hay bales into the loft at his farm.

One Sunday, it happened: The choice of an unwanted hymn was announced. John presented his glare. The hymnal slam echoed just as intended. The hymnal jam commenced on stage.

Except on this particular Sunday, John succeeded in ripping off the entire hymnal rack in his liturgy of displeasure. The wooden pieces clattered and rattled to the floor like a crescendo of Lincoln Logs gone psychotic.

It got really quiet in the sanctuary. Our musicians held in place. Our song leader's hands were frozen in space.

John did not know what to do or to say, but I did.

I leaned into the pulpit microphone, and in my best pastoral voice declared, "John, that wasn't one of the chosen twelve, was it?" I still consider my words to have been as gracious as they could be.

10

WHATCHA GONNA DO?

"I will sprinkle clean water on you, and you
will be clean; I will cleanse you from all your
impurities and from all your idols."

—*Ezekiel 36:25 (NIV)*

DOES YOUR FAMILY HAVE A TRADITION OR TWO? MAYBE
cutting off the end of the ham so the meat fits a pan no
one uses any longer? Or a certain mayonnaise brand that
must be purchased and enjoyed, and no other brand will
do? Perhaps a particular hamburger joint has to be visited
because the French fries are so much better than the other
places.

For the family in this story, the tradition was using
water from the River Jordan for baptisms. But not just any
water from Israel.

No, this water had been brought home in a large plastic
bottle long before September 11, 2001, and the restrictions
on liquids was put into place. Then, after the baptism

ceremony, the water was to be replaced in the plastic bottle so it would be ready for the next occasion.

Have you seen water from the River Jordan? It looks very much like water from most creeks around here unless it has been strained through multiple layers of cheesecloth.

Their water had not been cleansed to that degree.

He was the acolyte for the time of morning worship. He was trained in the art of taper-lighting and extinguishing. He was also skilled in assisting the clergy when a particular Sunday included the sacraments of baptism and holy communion.

Sunday morning came, bright and fresh. I arrived at the church building for Sunday school. Following that time of bible lessons, I made my way back to my office to prepare for worship, which would include a baptism with the family's treasured water.

I was passing by the men's bathroom when I heard an unusual noise from inside. It was the acolyte for the morning. The noise came as the man was emptying the metal bowl from the baptismal font into the sink.

I asked him what he was doing. He commented that the water for the morning's baptism was "kind of yucky" and needed to be replaced.

I asked where he got the water that he was pouring out.

He casually answered, "It had been in a two-liter Sprite bottle in the Sanctuary. When I walked in the bottle was being emptied by the family into the font. Like I said, it did not look clean."

My face is not made for poker or Go Fish. I am pretty sure I wheezed and gasped while grabbing for something to keep me upright. I recovered enough to check my watch. We had time before worship to work a New-Testament miracle of sorts. We would not be attempting the water into wine, but a much easier feat.

God had designed our building with a side door to the outside play area. That door was just around the corner from the bathroom, where I was still deep in prayerful shock.

I told the acolyte to rush out that door and get some dirt and a few leaves. He did.

Using my recollection of the coloration and density of Jordan River water, I prepared a metal bowl of water that was as close to the contents of that Sprite bottle as humanly possible.

It was then time for the swearing of "the oath." That oath consists of words to the effect that we will both perish and die in flames of agony if anyone ever finds out what we had done.

I put a heavy emphasis on *we*, because I wanted my friend, the acolyte, to be as fear-struck as I was. It seemed to work. We went about our duties and privileges of worship leadership that included as sweet a service of baptism as ever I conducted.

After all the photos were taken and the appropriate words were spoken, I got to that Sprite bottle and that baptismal font as quickly as I could.

I managed to pour some 98.97 percent of that "Jordan River" water back into that bottle and get the cap back on.

With great joy, I handed the water to the family as we all headed for the doors to leave the building. A mission that seemed impossible was accomplished.

Cue the theme music!

11

THE TIMING OF GOD

"This was now the third time ..."
                              —*John 21:14 (NIV)*

PLEASE CHECK YOUR HANDY-DANDY FUNKY-WAGGY BIBLE Concordance and you will find that the number three appears some 467 times in the scriptures.

Let that sink in. Most often, the number signifies harmony, new life, and completeness. Not always ... but most often.

I had been pastor to a congregation long enough to know that, on a clock, when the small hand is on the eleven and the large hand is on anything close to fifty-five, it is time for the closing hymn and the benediction.

One particular Sunday, the text for that day was a healing account from the gospel. Jesus was offering hope and mercy and grace to yet another person who was afflicted and conflicted by suffering. I love when Jesus does that. He had done that in my life on numerous occasions.

I decided to take a risk. Immediately following the

sermon, I announced an altar call for anyone who wanted to pray for someone he or she knew who was suffering. I knew we had lots of time to do this, to receive the morning offering, to sing a hymn, and to go in peace.

To my surprise, lots of people stood and moved toward the altar where I had several teams of "pray-ers" ready to kneel with them. I say this was a surprise because I (of course) thought knew everyone present who was carrying a burden for someone who suffered.

The hands of the clock moved way forward toward the exiting hour. Still, they came.

Then, as clearly as I type now, the Holy Spirit moved me to words. I gave a second altar-call invitation for people who needed prayer for themselves and their own suffering.

Again, I arrogantly thought I knew the two who would be making their way down toward me. Wrong! Again, the altar area was filled as the "pray-ers" knelt and listened and prayed. After the altar area was clear, I noticed my treasurer pointing to the bulletin to remind me that we had not received the offering.

I stepped toward the table where the offering plates rested. I reached to pick them up and to call the ushers forward. But again, I sensed the presence of the Holy Spirit.

The clock was screaming that it was now some twenty minutes past the magic hour of twelve. I tried my best to argue with the leading of the Spirit by reminding myself that everyone who had needed prayer for healing was now seated and ready for tithes and offerings, but the Spirit was gracious but firm. "You are to issue a third invitation for healing. And your words are to be clear and concise," it said.

I reluctantly agreed. I stood, facing the congregation, and said, "This is the third invitation for healing. Would someone come?"

No one moved for a few long seconds. Then one person stood. The individual made their way to where I was standing. They knelt. I leaned down and asked how I might pray with them.

Their words were clear. "I was wounded years ago and have never sought healing. I made a deal with God. I would not invite healing until someone used the words *third invitation*. You did, and here I am."

I do not remember being able to see much more than the face and the heart of the one in front of me. My prayer was one of praise and thanksgiving and gratitude to God for love and mercy and grace.

Do you know someone who is waiting? Perhaps it is time.

12

LETTERS AFTER YOUR NAME

"Come what may," he said, "I will run."
—*2 Samuel 18:23 (ESV)*

THERE SEEMS TO BE A LIST OF THE PEOPLE WHO ARE MOST IN demand to congregations, districts, and annual conferences. It is a quiet list, but I have heard about it. Other nonlist people can be invited, but it happens rarely.

You can imagine my delight and surprise when I was invited to be the keynote speaker at a men's conference on a Saturday in the fall. The first thing for me after I said yes was to check my calendar. Only the Raging Sand Fleas of State were not scheduled for a most-important football game during that weekend; however, I had already said yes.

What was I to address in my talk? Was I to encourage these men? Was I to instruct these attendees? Was I to challenge this conference?

I decided to drop back to my favorite Biblical home field stomping ground of telling stories about my life and about the peace and grace of God.

On the weekend of the conference, the attendance was underwhelming. The refreshments were excellent. The worship music was honest and rich. The introduction for me was short and sweet. There was an air of expectancy and delight that filled that sanctuary. Those in attendance had enough room so that any and all "social distancing" requirements were fulfilled and then some. Yet, we were one body for that time and space.

I reached *waaaaay* into my story memory bank. I told my best for them, beginning with humor and then moving to Jesus, and then to being a disciple, and then to "so what."

Although there were a few men who were "resting in the Lord" while examining the insides of their eyelids at the same time, most of the men were attentive and respectful of my stories. All, that is, except for the two youngest guys in the crowd. They were on the very front row, right in my line of sight no matter where I looked. They were also unable to be still or to quit wiggling around. The longer I spoke, the worse they got.

Some of you know that I would have been given some designating letters way back in grammar or middle school, if the current system of diagnosis had been in place. The letters chosen for me would have included a couple of *D*s, an *A*, and an *H*.

Being an educated and yet ignorant man, I had already determined that these two young men probably had some of the same letters associated with their names.

I was amid my last story. It was meant to have been the big wrap-up and take it home finale of my talking.

I finished. I asked the musician to offer a spirited piece

of music that would close out the meeting. It was at that exact moment that the two young men stood up. They spoke to me.

"Did you mean what you said in those stories?" they asked. "Did you mean that the peace and the grace of God cover all the Bible, from start to finish? Did you mean these Bible stories belong to us because God loves us?"

I did not hesitate, but said, "Yes."

The first young man said, "Then, we have to run the aisles."

My face must have yelled out, "What?"

He said, "We have to run with this good news." And off they went.

The sanctuary was a perfect indoor track. It had long aisles and lots of room. So, they ran.

The rest of the gathering stood with the closing music and searched their brains and life-experiences for something similar or even close to what was happening.

The two men circled around and came by me again. As they did, I realized that they knew exactly how to respond to the overwhelming and outrageous peace and grace of God.

So, I jumped into the aisle and ran after them. It seemed like a run that was worthy.

It was!

"Rejoice always, pray continually, give thanks in all circumstances; for this is God's will for you in Christ Jesus."

—*1 Thessalonians 5:16–18 (NIV)*

I wrote the following section in June 1991.

Our son John Dylan was born on June 21, 1973, at Emory University Hospital. He was now graduating from Meadowcreek High School and moving into his own life away from us.

Today is June 21, 2020. It is also Father's Day. I found these words in a file folder and in my heart.

13

THANKS FOR THE YEARS

IT IS SIMPLY NOT POSSIBLE!

Seventeen years cannot already have passed since that bright June day when you were presented to us in a tightly-wrapped, pale blue blanket.

Now it is your high school graduation. I am not sure I want to let you go! And just what choice do I have?

I preach about letting go. Now, I must let you go. It is so different than preaching.

I teach about forgiveness. Now, I must trust that our love for one another will hold fast. It is different than teaching.

I am positive about life and about the hand of God in our lives. Now, I must release you to life and to God. It is different than being positive.

But it is time. John, I thank God for you.

I thank God that your birth was on the fourth anniversary of the day I was discharged from active duty in the US Army.

I thank God for all the affection, love, patience, wisdom, and our relationship of these seventeen years.

I thank God for every trial, error, fault, mistake, hurt, misunderstanding and mess-up ever between us.

You have overcome numerous obstacles and difficulties. You are a unique member of your graduating class.

You have touched human lives! You have made a difference!

You go into this next stage of life with my prayers, my hopes, and some of my dreams. But please, know this:

You go mostly with my thanks. I love you, John!

Your dad,

David

14

LET THE CHILDREN COME ...

"He frustrateth the devices of the crafty, so that
their hands cannot perform their enterprise."
—*Job 5:12 (ASV)*

WE USED TO CALL IT THE "CHILDREN'S SERMON."

My way was to have two cloth laundry bags available
for the children to take home. One bag was blue. The other
was red.

Each week, I alternated the color of the bags and then
selected a child to bring a bag back with something he or
she liked or treasured inside.

There were rules for this: No living being in the bag
unless Pastor David was notified prior to the worship time.
No poison or dangerous stuff in the bag. Even if you told
Pastor David. If the thing in the bag was dead, then it had
to have been alive in the last twelve hours. This was like
the varsity.

Those were just about all the rules.

On Sundays, at the appointed time, I would invite all

the children to join me at the altar of the sanctuary. The child who brought the bag would sit next to me and then hand me the bag. I would open that bag and tell a story about the object or the stuff inside. The story was not necessarily true, but it was always accurate.

Over the years, I opened those bags to a myriad of surprises. All to the delight of the children. My all-time favorite was the Sunday I invited a magician to bring his own bag and present something about God during the children's sermon. It happened at the early time of worship, which was 8:45 a.m.

He was Steve the Magician. He was available for birthday parties, backyard soirees, wedding-anniversary entertainment, and last-minute presentations to save the hide of a forgetful parent.

Steve met me and the children at the altar. His first offering was a giant coloring book. The pages were filled with line drawings of famous Bible stories. He held the book so we could see that there were only outlines of characters and settings.

He then said some words about the colors of God's world. As he turned the pages of the book for the second time, the line drawings were all filled with magnificent colors, so the stories seemed to pop out at us.

The children were wide-eyed. I thought, *Good stuff!*

Next, he held up a giant domino with spots all over it, just like a real double-six tile. He said the same sort of words, but this time the story was about a large cat and its spots. It was accepted as biblical.

Steve rotated the giant domino while moving his fingers

and thumbs. This resulted in what appeared to be a series of different numbers as he turned the domino over and over.

The children's mouths were wide open in surprise. I thought, *Excellent!*

My seminary friend C. R. Hill used to explain complex Bible stuff while we sat at Hortons near Emory, waiting for the world's greatest short-order cook, Charlie, to prepare our feast of foodies. C. R. drew the answer to all things that were theologically confusing on a napkin with his pen. I wish I had saved those napkins and published them.

C. R.'s finale was always the same. He would use the phrase "pièce de résistance" to let us know that he was quickly summarizing the major point of some theological giant so we could scurry up the hill to class.

Well, Steve the Magician now announced his own "pièce de résistance."

This time there were no words spoken. I realized they were not needed. Using both hands, Steve held up a bright-red velvet bag. We were invited to look at the bag carefully to see that there was nothing up his sleeve.

While the children were busy trying to look up his sleeve, I noticed a slight bit of movement in the side of the bag.

I thought, *Whoaaaa!*

Steve then opened the bag. To his audience of mesmerized children and one stunned pastor, he took out a pure white dove and let it perch on this hand.

It was then that it happened.

In a voice that could be heard all over the building, one

child loudly proclaimed, "How did you do that?" and then pretended to faint.

I could not help myself. I also fell over and just lay on the floor in laughter.

The children were somewhat more divided in opinion. Some burst into wonderful giggles. Some others stared at the laughing child and me. My favorite response was from the parents of the "fainting" child, who were sliding lower and lower out of sight in their pew.

Would you believe how quickly the word of Steve the Magician and the dove spread throughout Cobb County? The sanctuary was packed with a huge standing-room crowd for the 11:00 a.m. worship time. Sadly, you cannot force love or forgiveness. Even sadder, you cannot force a magician to redo what was presented earlier.

Years later, I was at the end of my first sermon in the congregation to which I had just been appointed.

I saw a tall young-adult man standing around as if he was waiting to speak with me about some brilliant aspect of my sermon. Instead, he shook my hand and quietly said, "How did you do that? It was me, Pastor David."

And so he was. And so it was. And so it shall be.

15

JUST WHEN WE NEED IT

"Let us have confidence, then, and approach God's throne, where there is grace. There we will receive mercy and find grace to help us just when we need it."

—*Hebrews 4:16 (Good News)*

EVERY MORNING, KENNY WAS DOG-COLLARED AND CHAINED under the porch of the sharecropper shack in Florida. He was put there to keep him out of the sight and sound of his family. He learned to be invisible.

Something inside Kenny's heart and soul would not be defeated, even if his food was table scraps and no words of love were ever thrown in his direction. Only by his own stubbornness and the grace of God did he grow to be an adult. Now off the chain but still heavily bound.

One day, someone at a country store mentioned an ad in a magazine. It included an address to which men in Florida would write if they wanted to hear from women in Georgia who were seeking husbands.

A person offered to write a letter for Kenny to a woman living on a farm in the country. It took weeks of waiting, but then, to his amazement, his letter was answered with a train ticket and a photo of Caitlyn. He hitched a ride to the train station and thus continued a journey unlike most of us could even imagine.

Her father drove the two-mule wagon to the train station to meet Kenny. But after seeing him in person, her father shoved her back on the wagon and headed for home. Having come this far, Kenny walked behind that wagon for the thirteen miles needed to arrive at Caitlyn's house.

He was not welcome. It was plain that he needed to go away. But her father finally relented. They became husband and wife. Kenny raised rabbits to sell. Caitlyn and her mother made quilts from any available scrap material and offered them around the community.

I met them the first Saturday that I was the new pastor of the Methodist church up the road from their house. Actually, I did not meet them; I just answered the parsonage phone. It was Kenny on the other end of the line.

"Preacher," he said, "The preacher always takes me to the rubbing doctor 'twict' a month on Saturdays."

Sleep was still lurking in my eyes and in my heart. I said, "Huh?"

"The rubbing doctor has my appointment at nine o'clock, and then we go to the grocery store."

By this time, I figured that he meant he needed and expected a ride to the chiropractor and then to do his grocery shopping. Stuff like this was never covered in any of my seminary classes.

56

I picked Kenny up at his house and we made our way to town in my car. It turned out that the twice-a-month trips were somewhere in my job description, but not the one the staff-parish committee draws up so that measurements can be taken on the effectiveness of my ministry.

Nevertheless, it was a ministry to which I said yes.

Then, one very cold, bitter winter morning, that same phone rang with Kenny sobbing on the other end. "She's dead, Preacher."

I made my way down the road and found that Caitlyn had simply passed away sometime in the night.

Kenny was broken. We planned a funeral to celebrate her life. That was one of the most painful services at which I ever officiated.

I don't know how much later I heard pistol shots coming from the church cemetery about a quarter of a mile from the house. That is not a sound you want to hear.

You would not worry about a shotgun or a rifle in hunting season, but a pistol is often very personal. It was Kenny. He had somehow managed to borrow a pistol and cartridges. He was standing over Caitlyn's grave and firing into the air.

I pulled into the church yard. Kenny was finished with the pistol. He said, "Preacher, you know how the army shoots over the grave when they bury someone?"

"Yes, I do."

"Well, I thought Caitlyn deserved the same."

You know he was right, don't you?

16

JUST LIKE A GOOD NEIGHBOR

"Drink no longer water, but use a little wine for thy stomach's sake and thine often infirmities."

—*1 Timothy 5:23 (KJV)*

SARAH'S MOTHER BELONGED TO A CONGREGATION THAT WAS opposed to drinking "spirits" of any kind. There is great wisdom in such opposition.

She lived in the house next to Sarah and James. She was a gracious woman who loved to cook like old-fashioned "stove magicians" used to do. She also had a bottomless, brick-lined, bored well with the coldest water you would want on a blazing July afternoon when you had been cutting grass.

If I had time, I would ride my Snapper mower across the road to Sarah's mom's yard and cut her grass. Officially, this was to be a good neighbor and to get a glass of that skull-tensing cold water.

Unofficially, she would always have a cake or three plus a pie or two just lying around, waiting to be sampled.

Sarah and her husband, James, were our "down-the-road-a-piece" neighbors. They were our good friends. They hosted an hours-long Rook-playing festival on most Friday nights at their house. It was down and mean Rook, but no one ever got cut or stabbed.

One Friday evening, we were about an hour into the game when Sarah's mom called on the phone. She asked if I was down at the house. And, if so, could she come over and talk to me? She arrived in about four minutes and called me out of the kitchen and into Sarah's dining room.

She waited a moment. Then collected her thoughts.

"Brother David, can I ask you a favor?" she asked.

"Of course," I said.

I was imagining some conversation about predestination or "once saved always saved" or about questions like, who did Adam and Eve's sons marry?

In a tiny, whispered voice, she said, "I have been having some heart and some digestive issues."

Hmmm, I thought.

At the time, I was neither her pastor, nor had I completed my doctoral degree. I sensed this was to be a far deeper conversation than either of those two required.

"My doctor had prescribed that I drink two fingers of Jack Daniels Black Label Whiskey mixed with my well water every night before I go to bed.

"Every night?" I asked. This was nothing like I had anticipated.

"I will not have that liquor in my house. James bought

59

me a bottle, and I keep it under Sarah's kitchen sink. That way, I can just ease over at night and take my medicine. Now, James and Sarah's fingers are just too skinny. Will you pour me out two of your fingers of that Jack Daniels so I can mark my glass for the future?"

Proverbs 19:20 (CEB) advises that we are to "Listen to advice and accept instruction, so you might grow wise in the future."

You know, I believe I could sense a certain growth in my wisdom that night.

17

THEY WERE IN AWE!

"But he did not know what he was saying, for
they were in awe."

—*Mark 9:6 (Aramaic Bible in Plain English)*

MISS AMY DROVE THE PIANO WHEN SHE PLAYED. SHE PUT
every bit of her soul and body into her playing. She expected
the piano to behave accordingly. If the thing had not been
extremely heavy and caster-less, it would have moved from
the sanctuary out into the parking lot and down the road
a ways.

My Sunday-night preaching wasn't so much, but the
music and the singing were.

Miss Amy had a friend named Sara who came with
her to our evening worship. Sara didn't play any musical
instruments, but she owned a small diner in town and
could hurt a stove/oven in the best Southern tradition.

Miss Amy was Methodist and did not apologize for it.
Sara was Holiness and was very quiet about it. I knew all

about the Holiness movement in the United States because I was in seminary, and I had studied such things.

I also knew that the people of that religious persuasion played excellent softball because I had attended games out in Doraville, Georgia, back in the day.

Rumor was that they also sang loud and spoke in tongues. Rumor was that some of them handled poisonous snakes and drank strychnine out of fruit jars. Rumor was that some of them were healers like right out of the New Testament book of Acts.

I graduated from seminary and moved to my first full-time appointment as the "pastor in charge." That expression must have been made up by very naïve preachers because the people in that congregation knew exactly who was in charge. It was not me.

Several years later, I moved once again to another congregation in Atlanta. This time, I had an actual secretary and an office with my name on the door. I also had a telephone with several extensions for the different people on staff.

One day, the phone rang. My secretary answered and then buzzed me on line two. She said, "It's a woman from one of your previous congregations. Her name is Sara." I gulped lightly. Not out of fear or dread, but out of sheer wonder because I knew I had never met Sara's ideals about a minister of the gospel.

I had always sung as quietly as I could on the back row of the choir, where the basses congregated and were confined, so I wouldn't cause trouble for the director. I had so much trouble just keeping my mouth from doing damage that speaking in another tongue was out of the question. I had killed a variety of snakes over the years and once had roasted one to eat over a campfire. I had read and even taught a class or two on some of the verses in the book of Acts.

I punched the right button to speak with Sara.

She said, "Pastor David, I don't know if you remember me, but this is Sara from your first church. I was Miss Amy's friend."

"Of course," I said. "You had that restaurant off the square in town and cooked up some wonderful food for me."

"Well, Pastor David, I have been diagnosed with bad cancer. They want to operate on me at South Fulton Hospital next Thursday morning at seven o'clock in the morning."

"Oh my goodness. I will certainly remember to pray for you."

By this time in my ministry, I had been in classes in pastoral care. I had taken a clinical where I served as part of the clergy staff at both a hospital and a retirement facility. I even knew all the intricacies of prayer lists and prayer chains.

Sara interrupted my catalog of qualifications that indicated I was well suited to pray for someone over the phone as they were looking at the approach of surgery for cancer. "Pastor David," she said, "God has laid it on my heart that you are to come to the hospital and be the prayer warrior who prays that God will heal me."

I asked who else would be there. I was assuming there

would be a delegation from her congregation in addition to one or two ministers from her church.

"Only you and my husband will be with me. If you can come ahead of the surgery time and pray me up, I will be at peace no matter what happens."

She paused before continuing. "But the Lord has revealed that you are to be His instrument of healing for me. Can you be there?"

I do not believe I ever breathed that hard at any time in my life before that telephone call.

"Yes. I will see you Thursday," I said.

My memory bank does not contain any detailed files of the rest of that morning.

I know I shaved and dressed and drove over to South Fulton and found Sara and her husband in the assigned room. The nursing staff was busy with all that is required for someone who is about to undergo lengthy surgery.

We made small talk as the minutes flew past. I am not able to recall what I prayed, but I did the best I could. Then Sara was gone to the operating suite.

I knew enough to know that the longer surgery goes, the worse the news may be when the surgeon finds you in the assigned waiting area. In Sara's case, it was several hours longer than we expected. Her husband and I agreed that it was not always a bad sign to go so far past the anticipated hour to be finished with an operation.

I had heard the surgeon's shoes when he left the room much earlier in the day, before the surgery began. Now, I heard those same shoes approaching the room again—but this time, they were moving much faster than before.

The door opened. He entered the room.

"I know this has been way longer than you thought it would take. But I had to be sure. We went through every part of your wife's body where we had found cancer in the earlier diagnostics and biopsies," the surgeon told us.

We waited.

"There is no sign of any cancer anywhere in her body. I cannot explain what happened."

He shook our hands and made his way to more of the hospital.

I believe that I prayed to thank God for his healing mercy. At least my words were aimed in that general direction. After our goodbyes in the parking lot, Sara's husband and I went our separate ways. There was a profound silence in my car as I drove home. It sounded like awe!

18

WHAT A FELLOWSHIP, WHAT A JOY DIVINE!

"And Peter, not knowing what to say, said …"
—*Luke 9:33 (David Bowen adaptation)*

WHAT HAPPENS IN A NURSING HOME AT THANKSGIVING? A lot of the staff have to work. Many residents have no place to go and no one with whom to share the holiday. The chaplains also stay.

The *five* of us were serving as chaplains as we did what is called a "clinical" at the Wesley Woods Complex near Emory University. Wesley Woods is a wonderful ministry of the United Methodist Church in North Georgia.

There is one building for apartment living with optional meals in a dining room. Another building is for residents who need all their meals provided and nursing care available as required. There is also a third building with around-the-clock nursing care.

We five were assigned to provide chaplain ministry to the

entire facility. However, our primary area of responsibility was Budd Terrace, which is the middle building that invites residents to be somewhat independent.

Allow me to introduce you to the cast of characters who were called "chaplain" for the season from late summer to dead of winter in that memorable year: There was Pete, who was gifted in playing twelve-string guitar. There was Joel who juggled—no, really. He also loved to sing the classics like "Be Thou My Vision." There was David—the other David—who whipped any and all newcomers in Ping-Pong. There was Jerry, who hated to lose at anything, particularly at Ping-Pong. And then there was me, the other David, who was pastoring two United Methodist congregations in rural Henry County while serving as chaplain with these guys.

We limped and jumped and floundered and learned and grew while getting to know and love the residents and the staff of Wesley Woods. As the weather grew into fall, we began to realize that Thanksgiving would not be much of a celebration for the folks who would not be visited by family or be able to go home for a few days.

Since all five of us would be on-site for Thanksgiving, our conversations turned to the possibility of having a time of worship as part of the long weekend from Thursday through Sunday. We had musically talented people. We had guys willing to greet and welcome and serve. We had me with "sacramental privileges." That meant I could prepare and consecrate and serve holy communion in a service.

Excellent. We all agreed and signed and sealed the deal.

Now, for the bread and the wine. The bread would be

honey and whole wheat, made from a recipe that I received during a retreat at the Monastery of the Holy Ghost near Conyers, Georgia. The recipe made twelve small loaves. A cross would be cut into the top of each loaf to bring the symbol of Jesus's sacrifice for us right into view. I swooped by the huge kitchen and made arrangements with the chef for the bread to be ready and able for the time of worship. The wine would be from an ancient Methodist recipe that had been developed by a man named Welch. It was nonfermented grape juice. We even had a wonderful secretary in the chaplain's office who agreed to get the bottles of Welch's that we needed.

Everything was perfect. The communion elements were ordered. Our musicians practiced their music. The greeters fine-tuned their greetings and welcomes. The invitations were distributed to everyone who might be able to attend.

The day finally arrived. We opened the doors to a large auditorium on the ground floor of Budd Terrace. The five chaplains were on board and ready. We were blessed as residents and staff began to file in. Many were walking. Some were using canes and walkers. Some were in wheelchairs. There were even a few family members who decided to share the time of worship with people they loved.

Pete played. Joel juggled. David and Jerry greeted residents. I schmoozed like the middle child I am. Then it was the appointed hour. We had fellowship time. We had a hymn or three. We had prayers. We had scriptures read. I stood, facing the gathered people with my back to the table where the communion elements had been placed and then covered by a large drape. Then we began those gorgeous words of institution: "The Lord be with you ..."

I had not turned toward the communion table until it was time to remove the cover and consecrate the bread and juice. But as I turned, I noticed that the covering on the table looked like it was hiding a Volkswagen beneath it.

Seriously. Honestly. Really.

I invited help in removing the cloth, and when the table was revealed, there was a stunned silence in the room. There was also a guffaw or four. Then there were giggles and laughter. No one had ever seen anything like this!

It was later revealed that the chef had heard I wanted twelve recipes of twelve loaves of bread. Someone do the math. We had 144 small loaves of honey and whole wheat bread. It was also further revealed that the chaplains' secretary had heard that I wanted a dozen bottles of Welch's juice.

Looking back, I now celebrate that everything about the service was in twelve's, which is a good biblical number. But I digress.

Back to the Thanksgiving service.

I looked way inside myself for a word to say in inviting the collected people to receive the body and the blood of Jesus. But I was temporarily like the old guy who said he searched his brain for something with which to take mental notes but found nothing.

Then it happened. I said, "I have very good news. There is enough of Jesus to go around!"

That's right. Plenty of Jesus for us all.

19

MY MOTHER MADE A DELICIOUS ENGLISH TRIFLE

"Hear parents, your child's instruction, and forsake not your children's teaching, for they are a graceful garland for your head and pendants for your neck."

—*Proverbs 1:8–9 (ESV, with David Bowen adaptation)*

IT WAS ALL JOHN WESLEY'S FAULT.

After all, the bishop had asked us Wesley's "historic questions."

This is my paraphrase of the words toward ordination, but they are close. "Will you refuse to trifle away time when you are a pastor of a congregation?"

Our church buildings were located in the middle of a rapidly growing census tract. We had new members and needs for new stuff almost every week. How was I supposed to keep up with each and every personal detail? No trifling.

I had made a previous commitment to deliver meals on wheels on Tuesdays to about seven families. Summertime came, and our son John was available to hang with me on that particular day. John was only eight years old at the time, but he was eager to hang out with me on these food deliveries. I very maturely gave him the do's and the don'ts of the ministry. At least, I told him what I thought was required: We deliver as quickly as we can. We do not tarry with long conversations about this and that. You take the liquids, and I will handle the meals. Got it?

I was as smooth as a pastor trying to be all things to all people and to do them in a hurry. John Wesley would be pleased. Right?

One of our stops was to deliver food to the Brown brothers. The two of them had first names. However, under my rapid-delivery method, they were simply known as the Brown brothers.

We turned off the main highway and onto a smaller paved road. Then we drove down a long dirt driveway and up to the house. John grabbed the milk, while I got two meals, including bread, out of the cooler in the back seat of my car. I think our record for a two-person at one-household delivery was about thirty-two seconds. I knew we could be minimally friendly and also get the job done without a single trifle in sight.

My way of doing this went smoothly for the first two or three Tuesdays with John. Then he messed it up.

"Dad," he asked, "Don't you like the Brown brothers?"

"What?" I asked.

"Well, we run in and out of their house so fast that I

never get to know anything about them. Besides, aren't we supposed to visit with them since you said they live there by themselves and they don't go out much?"

"Well ..."

I made a decision. The very next Tuesday when John and I turned off the main highway and onto the smaller paved road, I shared that decision with him.

"We are going to get the milk and the food to take up to the house like we always do. But we are going to ask the Brown bothers if we can sit at their kitchen table and visit for a while," I told him.

We did. The room where we met and ate seemed lighter.

20

OUR FRIEND RUTHIE GEVA HAS DIED

"God brought you to this country to enjoy its fruit and bounty. (And this woman will teach you.)"

—*Jeremiah 2:7 (David Bowen adaptation)*

"YOU AMERICANS NEVER PRONOUNCE ANYTHING correctly!"

"Oh yeah! Like what?"

"You like to sing 'Hosanna' during worship around Palm Sunday and Easter."

"So?"

"The word is actually made up of four small Hebrew words and should be pronounced *Ho She An Na*."

"Oh."

If she was right about this simple word of ours, then what on earth were we to learn from this woman? It turns out these twenty years later that we were going to learn anything we wanted to ask her.

Her name is Ruti Geva. We transliterated it to Ruthie Geva because we just don't pronounce anything correctly— much less spell it.

- Archaeologist.
- Nature lover.
- Friend.
- Soldier.
- Defender of Israel.
- World traveler.

My favorite thing about Ruthie is her ability to tolerate senses of humor like mine. Not everyone has that gift. Another one of my favorite things about Ruthie is her willingness to invite and to spend hours answering questions that we normally are afraid to ask. She also has a piercing "Beeeeeeleeeee" that she squeals as she spots my wife, Billie, anywhere in the Holy Land.

Ruthie has a joyous love of music, especially any music that invites worship. She also offers to quote the words of Jesus in Hebrew as I break the bread and pour the wine in the Upper Room in Jerusalem.

Of all the things I love about Ruthie, my absolute favorite is what happens after we struggle through the precious "passport control" mass-herding things and get our luggage. Once safely on the other side of bureaucracy, we finally meet her as she screams, "Beeeeeeleeeee," while the rest of our party stands sort of speechless.

We meet our driver and collect our brains after the long trans-Atlantic trek. Then it happens. We have left America. We have prepared to be tourists after Jesus in the land He walked and loved.

But Ruthie has a better idea—for the rest of our time with her and for the rest of her life. We shall be her family.

And so it was. And so it is. And so it shall be.

21

GERMS IN THE COMMUNION CUP

"I will lift up the cup of salvation and praise
the LORD's name for saving me."

—*Psalm 116:13 (NLT)*

CAN MEMBERS OF A CONGREGATION ENJOY PIZZA AND
watch movies on the same night? Our group of young
adults didn't do this on the grounds or in the buildings
of the church, but they met monthly and engaged in such
behaviors. Billie and I joined them at their invitation. We
were apparently the fulfillment of the biblical admonition
to "honor the old people."

Besides Billie and me, Sandy and Jack were the only
married couple among the group. They celebrated a
headstrong relationship and marriage, with Jack usually
heeding Sandy's wisdom and advice on most matters,
except for that matter of the chalice or cup used in holy
communion.

Jack had apparently been attacked by vicious flesh-eating germs when he was a small child. Or he suffered from the trauma of seeing Lamprey eels in a nightmare based somewhere north of Kentucky. Or perhaps he just thought children should be neither seen and nor heard as part of worship. Especially on the Sundays on which we celebrated the Lord's Supper.

It would have been fine if we used only the small, plastic throw-away cups and the rock-hard, square-ish bits of dough as our communion elements. Yet, wanting to appear way cooler and more "happening" than I ever was, I, on occasion, would bring out the ceramic or metal cup and celebrate communion by "intinction."

That literally means to tear off a piece of the bread and to dip it into the cup and then partake of the two elements at the same time. You may be familiar with the regifting that children offer when the piece of bread they are grasping slips and slides back into the common cup. They have none of the fears that many of us adults tote around in great numbers. They may be afraid of something under their bed or in the closet, but "hand-fishing" for that semifloating piece of the represented body of Jesus does not faze them at all.

It happened one Sunday after Jack had been loudly and unceasingly teaching and upset about the profound effect of germs that the hands of the children in our congregation carried. In other words, he was about to go off the deep edge of fear and trembling about this matter of microbial infestation caused by the ones so dear to Jesus's heart.

Part of my duties as the senior pastor of the church on

that Sunday was to ensure that lights were off, the heat/ air thermostats were properly set, and that the front doors of the sanctuary were locked and secured. Billie and I complied with such duties. Once outside, I turned back toward the building to lock the doors.

It was then I heard them. Well, not *them*. But I heard Sandy in a voice that any drill sergeant would be proud to possess. She had Jack by the lapels of his suit coat. She grasped one lapel in each fist. She had drug him off the sidewalk over into one of the flower beds. He was paying close attention to her.

She said, "Jack, If the blood of Jesus can clean you up, then the germs of those precious children will not matter."

I smirked. I gave my wife the finest fist-pump ever seen outside any sanctuary on Jimmy Carter Boulevard.

Billie and I simultaneously whispered, "Yes!"

22

LEAVING ON A JET PLANE ...

"Where can I go from your Spirit? Where can
I flee from your presence?"

—*Psalm 139:7 (NIV)*

I HAD WORKED FOR FIVE YEARS TO ARRANGE AN EXCHANGE
with an English Methodist pastor and his family. My then
wife, my son, John, and my daughter, Lesley, were to leave
Marietta, Georgia, and fly to Cottingham, England, for
the summer.

Rev. John Beardsley and his family were to leave
Cottingham and fly to Marietta for the summer.

We were to leave our everything behind for each other:

- Our houses,
- Our cars and pets, and
- Our yards and congregations.

The lay leaders of John's congregation and mine were
in charge of all the arrangements. In May of that year, just

as we were really starting to get ready for the trip and the summer, I noticed that my wife was acting strange and was more distant than usual. I decided to ask how much the baby weighed—that is, I did not stop with my questions until about 3:30 the next morning.

It was then that she said, "When we return in early September, my parents will meet me at the airport. I will leave you and the children for good."

It took me a week to believe her, but I came to.

I began to dismantle the trip and cancel everything I had worked for five years to prepare, until I thought in my heart about what I wanted to do: I sold her plane ticket. I cancelled all the things we had scheduled to do that were in only her area of interest. I felt bold. Strong. Empowered. Ready, willing, and able.

We signed our no-fault divorce papers on a Friday. On Monday, John and Lesley and I boarded the 747 to Heathrow Airport near London and buckled in. John was eleven years old. Lesley was five.

I was bold. Strong. Empowered. Ready, willing, and able—until the kids had their Walt Disney meals that I had arranged in advance.

The flight was not full, so I was able to get them both a place to lie down and stay buckled in so they could sleep. I sat watching them sleep. When the rarely sought and often-avoided-until-the-last-minute thing known as reality found me.

In England, I had

- No family,
- No friends,
- No support,
- Was in a new country,
- Had a new house,
- Had a new car driven on the wrong side of the road, and
- Did not have a familiar anything anywhere, and who did I think I was?

I had made reservations near London at a bed and breakfast. We took the train from the airport into London. From there, I got a cab for all our gear and us. We arrived in the Hammersmith section of London and found our lodging.

Angus and Anika Goodwill met us at the front door. They said, "We thought there were four of you."

We talked while the children had a long nap before supper. It turned out that Goodwill was not just their name. The goodwill of God permeated every part of their lives as a family. My children and I were cared for and blessed and graced and loved as if we were their family whom they had not seen for a while.

The whole week in London, I was preparing my speech to explain my wife's absence. Have you ever prepared a speech for a situation when you had no earthly idea what you were doing? I decided to leave as scheduled and travel up from London almost to York, where we were to be met at the train station by the lay leader of the Cottingham Methodist Church.

The train slowed and stopped at the station. I did a double take because a man who was the very image of my uncle Dan of Rome, Georgia, was holding up a sign with our names on it. We introduced ourselves. His name was Ian.

He and his wife, Jean, shared duties and ministries as lay leaders of the congregation. He said we were to go to his home, where the staff parish relations committee was anxiously waiting to meet the American pastor. I gulped a great gulp. He never once asked why there were only three of us and not four.

When we arrived, it was time for tea. Jean suggested my children go down the hall a bit and join her own children, who were almost the same age as John and Lesley.

I took another large gulp. The English can chat pleasantly for quite a while and not get to the rhinoceros in the room. Finally, Ian asked about the change in plans, changes for which they had not prepared, and changes that threw all of us, he was certain.

I told my story. As I finished, I said, "We have enough money to return to London and stay a while. You did not prepare, and you are not prepared for a broken, divorced man with two children to serve your congregation for a summer."

We sat for a few minutes in a time of prayer with no one speaking. But we were all praying the same prayer. They asked me to step down the hall and join the children for a bit. They would call me when they were ready for me to rejoin them. My gulp was so loud.

Ian returned and invited me back into the room. As I sat down, I realized the Lord was in that place and that they had known it all the time. I had not. Just as God had gone before us to England and to that congregation, God was with us in that room.

The chair of staff parish spoke. He said, "David, we were a congregation of believers some forty years before you became a nation. You will not be the worst pastor who has ever served here. On the other hand, you will not likely be the best, either. We believe that God meant for you and these children to be here among us for this time. God has prepared the way for both John Beardsley and you to live this wonderful exchange. We are asking that as best as you are able, you minister to our people. You preach and teach, you visit, and you be our pastor. We know how to be the church." Then he said, "Let us pray."

And thus began our summer in Cottingham.

23

REMINDERS THAT WE ARE NOT IN CHARGE

"Our mouths were filled with laughter …"

—*Psalm 126:2 (NIV)*

THERE WAS A TIME BEFORE WE BECAME SO SENSITIVE TO language that I could write the actual words here as they appeared in several worship settings.

For instance:

The officiant used to ask someone representing the bride's family: "Who is giving this woman to be married to this man?"

The father of the bride was the one chosen to speak. He paused a moment. Then he looked right into my eyes and said, "What do you mean? This is costing me an arm and a leg."

I looked right back into his eyes, and I said, "Thank you. You may rejoin your family as you are seated."

For instance …

My understanding of a "flower girl" was a child who strews the petals of flowers as a way to prepare for the bride. However, a family member from out of town decided that this particular flower girl would be given two dozen long-stem red roses to cast on the carpet as a "bride incoming" sign.

Things went well as the first two or three roses were carefully laid in the aisle. But then the flower-strewer was visited by a meanness of some kind that convinced her the roses could be launched like a guided missile. Not only could they be launched, but they were.

No one seated in the sanctuary knew whether to laugh out loud or to be upset at this display of prenuptial behavior. So, no one did or said anything as the throwing and ducking and dodging continued down the aisle—that is, until the flower distributor reached the pew where her mother was seated. Her mother's long arm snaked out of the pew, collected the flower girl, and pulled her out of sight into the full grasp of her maternal care.

There followed several hand-blows (i.e., spankings) on the backside of the young child's lovely dress. After that, there was a moment of silence. Then the same long arm moved out of the pew to deposit the girl back into the aisle with a rather changed facial expression, whereupon, the flower girl correctly and carefully placed the remainder of the long stem red roses on the carpet.

For instance …

At a wedding, the officiant used to ask the gathered congregation, "If anyone can show just cause why this couple may not lawfully be joined in marriage, let them now speak or forever hereafter hold their peace." After this, usually, there might be a cough from the crowd, but rarely, if ever, would anyone actually use words.

Well, there was that one wedding. Since I was supposed to ask this question, I addressed those words and then was ready to move ahead with the remainder of the service. But it was then that the aunt of the bride stood up and said, "I have an objection."

I drew myself to full height and said: "What is your objection?"

Straight-faced, she said, "We don't like him."

After an appropriate stall to pray for five seconds, I said, "That is neither a lawful nor a legal objection. Therefore, you may be seated with your family."

For instance …

It was my first Easter Sunday in my first church. We had previously celebrated the Lord's Supper on the first Sunday of each month. Since an overflow congregation was expected for Easter, the altar guild supplied extra bread on a covered plate. They also left a cellophane-covered roll of small glasses so that I might fill them as needed. Which brings me to the juice that would fill them.

There was a cut-glass pitcher of grape juice that sat on the oak communion table. I was a brand-new preacher, but I was confident that I could place the glasses in the appropriate holes in the trays and fill them from the pitcher. No problem—and there wasn't, until I began to place the cut-glass pitcher back on the oak table. The table with the unbeveled edges.

That's right! I hit the edge of the pitcher on the sharp edge of the table.

There was a miracle for a moment. Time stood still as the bottom of the pitcher fell onto the floor of the sanctuary ultra-slow-motion. The grape juice was holding solid inside the rest of the pitcher, which was still, somewhat shockingly, in my hand. But then the laws of gravity began to seize the juice, and it sloshed onto the brilliant-white table linen and down my legs, into my shoes.

There was a loooooooong silence, but then—very softly at first, but rising into the sounds of a community at joy— the chortling and giggling and guffawing broke out. The joy even got me!

24

ONE SUNDAY IN LITHONIA

"Then I saw another angel flying directly
overhead, with an eternal gospel to proclaim
to those who dwell on earth, to every nation
and tribe and language and people."

—*Revelation 14:6 (ESV)*

HAVE YOU EVER BEEN PART OF A REVELATION CHURCH? NO,
not the name *Revelation*, but rather, a congregation made
up of many nations and tribes and languages and peoples.

More than twenty years ago, I was privileged to be part
of one. We had members and attendees from at least four
nations in Africa, from most of the Caribbean Islands, from
several countries in Central America, and from all over
the United States. I loved to hear that congregation sing
because the people were not able to disguise or to hide their
various accents and native voices as they sang.

I loved to share covered-dish meals with that
congregation because they brought dishes that were native
to their countries and cultures. Lord, have mercy on

some jerk chicken and plantains! I loved to be in worship with that congregation because many of them wore their traditional worship clothing from back home. I also loved to preach in that congregation because the majority were from a Wesleyan-faith background. They wanted to hear about the grace of God.

It happened that Sunday in mid-summer. Billie and I were closing up and securing the front/main doors to the sanctuary. I stepped out into the bright sunshine that was just outside those doors. It was there that I checked my hunger sensors to see if Matthew's fried chicken in Tucker, Georgia, was possible that day.

Then I saw him. A man was walking slowly up the sidewalk to the steps, atop which I stood. You know some of the things that run through your mind, don't you? They did that day.

He stopped about halfway up the steps and stood facing me.

"Hello," I said.

He replied the same and then was silent.

As surely as I am typing this on a Dell laptop, the Spirit of God or perhaps it was an overhead-flying angel that spoke to my spirit. Stepping back and holding open the doors of the sanctuary, I asked him if he wanted to come inside. I knew he did.

He said that he did, but …

I waited.

He said that he was not clean enough to enter the house of the Lord. I was stunned. In all my years of ministry, I had never heard those words from human lips. I felt like

Paul Harvey in his story of the birds that were just outside his patio lights on Christmas Eve.

What could I say or do to make him aware that everyone and all are welcome in God's house?

Billie had moved and was now standing beside me on the porch in the sunlight.

I asked the man how we could help him.

He said, "If I am baptized, then I can enter the Lord's house."

This situation was not covered in any of the classes I had in either seminary I attended or in my clinical. Or in my previous years of ministry.

Not knowing yet what to say, I said nothing. Again, the Spirit spoke to my spirit.

I said, "Would you like to be baptized now"?

"Yes," he said.

Turning to Billie, I asked her to go to the kitchen and bring us a pan or a bowl of water and a towel. The man and I stood as she quickly brought those things to us.

Many of you have heard or you know about the ancient words of that magnificent ritual of baptism. I asked the man about his trust in Jesus as his Savior and his Lord. I asked him about his desire to be baptized in that time and place. I asked him to kneel on the pavement of that porch. Then, announcing those words in the name of the Father and of the Son and of the Holy Spirit, I took a huge double-handful of water and released it all over his head and shoulders.

He screamed as if he had been shot and fell backward. He was not injured, but something was changed and moved and different in every molecule of the air around the three of us. I then knew that he was not going to enter the sanctuary. He had no need.

Turning, he began to walk away from Billie and me toward the street. And just out of my direct line of sight, just over in the edge of what I could see in that bright sunshine, I saw the flash of a wing.

And I know that I heard two words: "Beloved son!"

25

GETTING READY TO DISCIPLE

"Jesus said to them, 'Come away with me. Let us go alone to a quiet place and rest for a while.'"

—*Mark 6:31 (Worldwide English Translation)*

I ATTENDED A RETREAT AT LAKE JUNALUSKA, NORTH Carolina, a United Methodist Center. It was just like Epworth, by the Sea at Saint Simons, but it was in the mountains and not at the beach. The retreat leader invited us to find a quiet place and speak to Jesus. My response—well, my initial response—was, *say what?*

"No, seriously, really go to a place apart and speak with Jesus," the leader said.

"What do I say to Jesus?" I asked.

"That will be given to you. Now, go."

And I paid good money for this? I thought.

It is sometimes hard for me to focus—look, there's a squirrel. But I gave up fighting the plan and just did it. God gave me a vision. Not like John on the Island of Patmos, but a vision, nevertheless. In my vision, I was walking up an incline in the woods. I was alone but not anxious. I was also aware of a glow on the horizon in front of me like a sunrise that is just getting birthed. As I came closer to it, I began to see it was a campfire.

There was someone sitting in front of the fire. He someone invited me to sit down across the fire from him. I did. He was wearing a dark brown hoodie. I looked as hard as I could at him through the dancing flames. Lord, have mercy, it was Jesus.

He was pleasant. He asked me what I wanted from him. I tried to answer based on ambition and want and imagination and success and power and glory and big church and … then I was struck by the majestic simplicity.

Earlier in my life, I had received Jesus as my savior. I had also committed to following Jesus as my Lord. Why not ask him? So, I did.

"Jesus, what would you give me?" I said.

He said nothing for a long while. After that, he reached very slowly into the flames and the fire, but nothing was consumed. He took a double handful of fire and flame and shaped it roughly into a sphere like a blimp. He extended both arms toward me, the fire still in his hands, and offered it to me.

Talk about feeling out of your control and way beyond your comfort zone. I reached forward and took the flames. But again, nothing was burned or consumed by them. As I held the glowing, shape-changing, and color-rearranging mass, a form began in the fire. The form was that of a bare-naked baby boy. Then, the vague outline of the baby began to reshape again, and the face of the baby became *mine*.

The gift of Jesus was that I was a new creation in him. I was changed from shapeless and formless into a brand-new me. The word, in Greek, in John 3:3, is *anothen*.

Jesus said to Nick (Nicodemus) on that fateful evening, "Nick, you must be born *anothen*."

It means a lot:

- From heaven
- From above
- Again
- Anew
- From the top to the bottom

This is OK for Nicodemus, but why would Jesus do this to me? It's simple: so I could be His disciple.

Some people you tell that story, they say, "Yeah, he belongs to them." Other people you tell that story, they say, "Hmm. He belongs to us."

I would ask you to remember that David Bowen, he belongs to Jesus.

26

ONE EVENING NEAR ANSLEY MALL

"We had to celebrate and rejoice ..."
—*Luke 15:32 (The Complete Jewish Bible)*

HAVE YOU EVER WITNESSED THE JOY OF RECONCILIATION? My daughter, Lesley, and I have. She was just fifteen years old at the time. As often happens, a young woman whose mother has left the home will become every energized to find out the why behind her mother's leaving.

This particular scenario required that I insist Lesley leave our house if she was not able to live there and cooperate with my attempted parenting. We did not know this at the time, but it unfolded as was best.

Lesley moved into her mother's apartment in the heat of a Georgia August. I was about as broken in half as anyone has ever been. Time demanded the slowest passage of days and weeks as was allowable under the laws of grief and pain. Lesley and I rarely communicated with each other for all those long months that drug past her sixteenth birthday in January and toward the coming of the season of Lent in April.

I found employment out of town and I buried—yes, that word, *buried*—myself in work and pretending to have a life. I was about half right. Then one morning, it happened. Lesley called me on the phone. Her words were as prodigal as any words ever spoken.

"Dad," she said, "I cannot get on with my life if you are not in it."

If shock and awe of profound blessings can kill over a long-distance cell phone call, then I was dead at her words. Dead with hesitating joy and relief and heart-pausing disbelief and hope and ...

"When can we meet?" I blurted out.

"When would you like?" she replied.

"How about tonight? I can pick you up at six o'clock. I mean, if that's alright with you."

"Fine. See you then."

Old dude Andy Williams sang, "The Street Where You Live" as part of a song-track album from *My Fair Lady*. The words are for a couple who have been apart for a while and who want to see each other.

After work, I drove at light speed toward the street where Lesley lived. Nothing mattered except that I was going to be with her. Which scared me to death. What if? Suppose? What if?

I pulled into the parking lot behind her building and waited with breath that was so far beyond bated, it was fit for centuries instead of one eagerly anticipated evening. Then she joined me.

There were those hugs and that rush of tears and tears and tears. The words between them were what homecoming must be for a soldier or a traveler or anyone longing for home. Not really home as a place, but, well, you know, don't you?

Lesley slid into the passenger seat. "Where shall we go?" she asked.

I had no idea.

Thank God, I had heard that the Old Hickory House on Piedmont Road near Ansley Mall was now a wonderful restaurant that served good steaks. It was called Cowtippers. That's right.

We drove and talked over and around the months that hung between us as silent ghosts. At the door of the restaurant, I was as bold as I had ever been.

"This is my daughter," I said. "We are here to celebrate. We would like a table with your most patient and kind waitperson. We would like to be somewhat away from the crowd, as we will probably be weeping a lot. We don't want to disturb others. I will be tipping our person at least fifty percent for their service."

The doors of heaven could not have opened as wide. The staff offered smiles and "sirs" and "ma'ams" all over the place as they found the choicest of seats for us.

I had witnessed a few cow-tipping events in my earlier life, but the restaurant never brought such into sight.

Instead, there was salad. There were steaks, medium-rare, as the Lord intended. There were chocolate malts and pie for dessert and several hours between tears and so much laughter that the very air in the room seemed lighter for everyone else who was there that night.

Afterward, we drove back to Lesley's apartment's parking lot. We exchanged goodnights. As she climbed the steps to the building's outer doors, she turned for just a moment.

"I love you, Dad!" she said.

"I love you," I shouted off the walls of the adjacent buildings.

And somewhat away from the bright lights and just out of the direct line of sight of either father or daughter, there was a tiny presence that still calls itself grace.

27

IT'S ALL DOWNHILL FROM HELEN, GEORGIA

"Spread your bread on the water—after a while you will find it."

—*Ecclesiastes 11:1 (International Standard Version)*

DID YOU EVER MEET A REAL "WHEELER-DEALER" WHO WAS just all smooth as he tried to talk you into some kind of deal? I did. He came by my office to convince me that the canoes were not really stolen; they had just been taken from the private school without permission and would be returned as soon as the river trip was finished.

He waved his arms like a country preacher getting to the point as he described the proposed trip down the Chattahoochee River to the Gulf of Mexico in Florida. He said he would transport all his gear and the canoes to the mouth of the river, which begins north of Helen, Georgia. The proposed trip would then be a float through Columbus, Georgia, and south, finishing near Wewahitchka, Florida.

He said he would be shooting stills with a camera that he had borrowed so a collection of his photographs would be published. He would be filming with a movie camera that he borrowed so a film would be made of the trip. He also would be keeping a meticulous daily journal and that one of the Atlanta newspapers had already agreed to publish his story in a feature article.

The plan was airtight and as smooth and slick as a vegetable slicer salesman at a county fair. There was only one problem: What if he was stopped by law enforcement and asked about the ownership of these two canoes? He had that covered as well. He laid on my desk a legal-looking bill of sale. All I had to do was sign and date the thing so the canoes were his.

You see my problem, don't you?

That's right. I did not own the canoes in the first place. So, how could I sell them? Worse, that proverbial monkey would shift blame to my spine if problems arose.

I said no. He was not pleased, but he did not quit until every possible reason I had to refuse has been depleted. The truth is, I couldn't see that I would get anything out of the deal except a possible trial and conviction for breaking and entering and theft.

He left my office for greener pastures. You know he found them, don't you?

This brings me to my uncle Pete, or "Uncle Duck," as we cousins knew him.

Pete would have made an excellent model to be used in

a movie called *Secondhand Lions* if one of the two actors had called in sick. He was exactly that kind of character. You never knew what amazing story he would recall or what scavenger hunt he would invent to entertain the horde of very bored young relatives hanging around under the spreading live oaks at my Aunt Gloria's house near Panama City, Florida.

Pete loved to go fishing, and he was good. He was not quite as proficient as my dad, who always went "catching" as well as fishing. He loved the area down near Wewahitchka, Florida. It is difficult to reach that area by accident. You have to want to be on either the Dead Lakes or on the Apalachicola River.

If you check your map sites on your iPhone or computer, you will find that the Apalachicola River drains from Lake Seminole up in Georgia. You will also find that Lake Seminole is fed by the Chattahoochee River, which winds its way south out of the mountains in new Helen, Georgia.

This brings me back to the hustling canoe- and camera-borrowing man from Atlanta. I never saw the pictures or film or article in the Sunday paper as promised. I wondered what happened. How could a plan that smooth ever fail or come to trouble?

Then one day, he popped into my office building to chat with a friend. I joined them and heard the most bizarre story you have ever heard told. It seems that every detail of the trip came about as planned: the photos of the glorious Chattahoochee were being shot, the film was nearing perfection, and the daily journal entries were flowing with Pulitzer-winning appeal. The two paddlers crossed Lake

Seminole in their canoes with almost no headwind to slow them down. From there, they were on the final leg down the Apalachicola River to the Gulf.

The weather was perfect and the water was smooth as silk, until a strong weather front, complete with swirling winds, unexpectedly came up from the south and stopped them and all the fame that awaited them dead in the water about thirty-five miles from their destination.

The fame-seeking and wealth-anticipating canoe borrower stopped his story with tears almost snaking down from his eyes. My friend and I waited with bated breath. Actually, we did.

"Then the worst thing you could imagine happened to our trip. We met this old codger in a fishing boat with an eighteen-horsepower Johnson outboard motor. He asked if we would like a tow down to near Wewa, where he was parked, and then we could finish the few miles to the Gulf. It seemed like a great idea.

"The guy tied a rope from the back of his boat to the front of my canoe. I secured another rope to the second canoe. We were off to finish the trip so we could go home. The wind in our face got stronger and stronger, and the guy gave his motor all the gas he had to make any headway. Nobody knew that doing this would pull the front of the first canoe under the water. We yelled our brains out, but the old man could not hear a lick.

"That guy sunk both canoes and all our film gear and my backpack with my journal. They are all in the bottom of the Apalachicola River. And the guy did not even say he was sorry. He did take us and what gear we could salvage to the van that we had waiting at the landing."

This brings us to a Thanksgiving family gathering at my Aunt Gloria's house sometime later. Uncle Pete was in rare form. We were all spellbound for hours with his latest story.

It seems he was running in his fishing boat up the "Apalach" and met a couple of young men trying to reach the Gulf by canoe. He said they were so rude and arrogant and would not listen to anything he tried to tell them. They insisted that he tie their canoes to his boat and then take them down river.

Uncle Pete had the strangest grin as he finished the tale of how his offer to help two guys on some film trip resulted in their sinking the canoes with all their gear.

Yup. You can't make this stuff up. And if you did, it wouldn't be nearly as funny as the real thing. I sure do miss my uncle "Duck."

28

PLEASE DESCRIBE AN INSTRUCTOR FOR ME

"The instruction of the LORD is perfect, renewing one's life; the testimony of the LORD is trustworthy, making the inexperienced wise ... and more desirable than gold—than an abundance of pure gold ..."

—*Psalm 19:7, 10 (Christian Standard Bible with David Bowen adaptation)*

I LOVE THE OLD COLONIAL BREAD DOOR FIXTURES ON country stores in the south. I haven't seen one in a while, but it was fun to see them when I was coming and going as a child. Not so much with the modern version, though. They have morphed from advertising ingenuity to air-piston-driven door-slammers.

One of these been had installed on the front door of the parsonage furnished by the congregation to which I had just been assigned. Billie and I had just married. We thought that our four children would be better together in a house that was neither "theirs nor ours," and we were somewhat correct in that decision. So, we packed and moved.

Way back in high school, I fell in love with teaching. I was never so happy as when I learned that a preacher could teach and mostly stay out of trouble with members who thought being picky and grumpy were spiritual gifts. I knew they were actually the two missing dwarves from Snow White's adopted family.

One of my bible study classes in the congregation that we had just left gave me a brand-new ceramic chalice, a cup out of which I would serve holy communion. I carefully boxed it and secured it with bubble wrap for the move.

I was excited to find that we would be celebrating the Lord's Supper on my third Sunday in my new appointment. I unwrapped my new chalice and got it ready for the sacrament that always blesses so many in worship.

Sunday morning arrived. I was armed with my Bible, a sermon, and my chalice. I was easing out the front door of the parsonage when my brain did a forgetful thing. What it forgot was the lurking presence of the piston-driven door-slammer. Unfortunately, it worked perfectly.

I was given one of those special moments of prayer as I watched my new and unused chalice fall from my grasp and make full contact with the front steps of the house. I was speechless, which was probably a good thing.

When they birthed me, my parents had a child with too much desire for his own human perfection. Things like dropping ceramic containers on brick and concrete always bring out the best of deep misery and frustration in me.

That Sunday chalice-drop was a real heart crusher. It took a few minutes for me to realize that the pieces of that cup would not magically mend themselves like hitting rewind or reverse on some video equipment. It was also then that I figured, if I could not have the whole cup, I could at least sweep up and keep the pieces. So, I did.

I was miserable in my soul as I zipped up the large baggie of pieces and bits and put it away in a safe place. And I cannot honestly tell you how Barry Lawrimore found out about the broken chalice. But he did. He asked me if he could have the baggie of pieces. They were more like seven large chunks, a stem in half, a handful of fragments, and a sneeze or two of dust.

Sometime later, Barry presented me with my chalice. It was whole and complete and perfect. If you have any old wounds that have become beloved scars, you will know how the chalice felt and still feels. Never have such love and friendship and superglue met in this life!

It is now thirty-three years since the great chalice drop and healing. I use that precious cup a lot, especially when the people I am privileged to serve would appreciate a story about grace and scars. The word in Japanese is *Kintsugi*, which best translates as "golden joinery." This is the art of repairing broken pottery by mending the areas of breakage with lacquer or glue that are mixed with powdered gold.

I have a word in my heart for what happened so that

my chalice was restored and healed and mended and returned to a life of serving. It is not *Kintsugi*, and no was gold used in the mending. Instead, God used a friend named Barry.

Such a friend is more valuable and more precious than any gold!

29

MY FIRST SUNDAY
... AND THEIRS

"My brothers and sisters, think of the various
tests you encounter as occasions for joy. After
all, you know that the testing of your faith
produces endurance."

—*James 1:2–3 (Common English Bible)*

LORD, HAVE MERCY ON THE UNITED METHODIST
congregation that receives a new pastor after annual
conference, a pastor who has never preached a sermon
before. That would likely never happen now, but waaaaay
back then, it did.

On that first Thursday, I had done the obligatory drive
over to the church buildings to get the lay of the land. All
I saw was a white clapboard sanctuary building and a small,
stand-alone fellowship hall/Sunday school building. I saw
nothing about the lay of anything otherwise.

Then came my first Sunday as pastor. I had not yet met

anyone in the congregation. I had sort of compiled a stab at a sermon. I had run off the bulletins on a mimeograph machine that was so old, it could have been used in Ben Franklin's personal office. I had enough "pregame" in my nerves and my stomach to play an entire season of football. I told myself that I was ready.

The sanctuary sat back from the highway down a lovely tree-lined lane. It took a long time to drive those 162 feet, but I managed. The first thing I noticed was the haze of smoke that came from the knot of about sixteen men who were standing by the front steps of the sanctuary. I parked and walked toward them.

Roy stepped out a foot or two toward me and said, "You must be the new preacher."

I managed to agree with him while wondering just what that meant.

I said, "Yes, sir. I am David Bowen. It's good to see y'all this morning."

That helped, because I knew how to say *y'all.* In that section of the country, it is a blessing to speak at least some of the local language.

After that, it got still. I could see a few wasps and a couple of yellow jackets seeking some relief from the mid-June heat. The smokers took a drag. The Red Man chewers did what they were supposed to do. The other two guys assumed the traditional posture of waiting for the leadership to lead.

Roy led off. "Preacher, we got a question."

Oh, Lord, I thought, *It's a test. My first Sunday in the ministry and I got a test.*

"Preacher, you got a mule or a tractor that needs help getting unstuck and it's Sunday morning early. What do you do?"

I thought a while. It did not take long, because my tractor and mule experience was slender. Then my brain was visited by a Bible verse of long ago.

I said, "You got an ox in a ditch on the Sabbath, you got to get him out. That's in the Bible."

Every one of those men either took another drag or Red-Manned as they needed or nodded as if I had passed. In fact, I did.

I imagined that it was time to walk into the sanctuary, so I did. The first thing I noticed was a group of some twenty-five women who were standing near the piano to the left of the altar rail. I walked up toward them when one woman stepped a foot or two in my direction.

It was Clyde, who I found out was married to Roy. They had been married for a very long time. She said, "You must be the new preacher."

I managed to agree with her while now really wondering just what that meant.

I repeated my earlier line and said, "Yes, ma'am. I am David Bowen. It's good to see y'all this morning."

Again, that helped because I knew how to speak politely. In that section of the country, it is a blessing to speak in the proper tone of the local language.

Again, it got still. But Clyde did not wait for permission to lead.

"Preacher. We got a question," she said.

I thought, *My goodness, another test. And this one will be tougher.*

She said, "What do you think of wearing pants to church?"

I called on all the saints. I called on the Holy Spirit. I called on anyone who had ever said anything wise about what to wear to worship.

Finally, I thought, *Why not go with the truth?*

Out of my mouth came, "I plan to wear them every Sunday."

From the group of women, there were one or two smiles. There were even three or four light laughs. The rest of the faces indicated mild surprise.

As the women moved toward their seats and the men came through the front door to join them, I felt something inside that I can only describe as joyous relief. My first Sunday, and I passed! Thank the Lord!

30

WORDS TO SHOW MY HEART

"When my heart is weak, I cry out to you from the very ends of the earth. Lead me to the rock that is higher than I am."

—Psalm 61:2 (Common English Bible)

I KNEW HE WOULD CALL ME. SINCE HE HAD BEEN DIAGNOSED with cancer, we had met for food several times. Mostly to talk. But this phone call was going to be different.

I met Phil through a retreat experience called "The Walk to Emmaus." Every generation or so, God gives an experience for people that refreshes and renews and strengthens them in their seeking to follow Jesus. In our time, that event was the Emmaus Walk.

Phil and I also shared a room at several annual conferences, including that one in Athens when the room we used invited so much rain inside that we watched it run down the walls. He and I also got to share one trip to the Holy Land, Israel. Those ten days were like a good summer camp with God.

As Phil's cancer progressed, I made the drive from our home to his because that is what friends do. I noticed that he was framing his "goodbye" at the same time that I wanted him to stay.

Sometimes, when people have real clarity about the time they have left in this life, there is a peace over and around them that defies description. I noticed this peace as Phil was finishing as much earthly business as he could. One day he asked me if I would speak at his funeral. My mouth formed agreement though I began to dread the same gift and task that was set before me.

Later that month, he called. I believe in prayers that refuse to fit being highly structured.

Anne Lamott wrote a book on words to pray that is one of my favorites. It is titled *Help, Thanks, Wow*. But even her wonderful book could not give me the words I began so desperately to crave.

Have you ever done "steering-wheel praying"? I did that day as I sat in the driveway with my car refusing to start.

Truth is, I did not turn the key to make that happen. I sat maybe ten minutes. Maybe longer. Yet, the time comes when it is time.

The first obituary I wrote for myself was back in my clinical days with Joe and Dave and the Crew at Wesley Woods. In that obit, a musical group called "the Beatles" would be singing. Hey, that was a long time ago.

My newfound group to love and to sing at my funeral was Third Day. I had just gotten a copy of their newest CD. It was still wrapper-bound. The CD is *Wherever You*

Are. I pushed the disc into the player and began to drive. The first two songs came and went. So did the third song. Went it did—straight into my crying out to God for heart and soul relief.

The song is titled "Cry Out to Jesus." It opens just like this: "To everyone who's lost someone they love long before it was their time ..."

The waves will one day be overwhelming. The winds will blow fiercely. The storms will come. You are going to need a rock onto which you can hold. Or better, a rock that will hold you in the storm.

"In nomine Patris et Filii et Spiritus Sancti..."

Amen.

31

THE FRIDAY BEFORE
THAT FIRST SUNDAY

"My command is this: Love each other as I
have loved you."

—*John 15:12 (NIV)*

IT IS FRIDAY IN THE EARLY AFTERNOON. IN TWO DAYS, I
will preach my first sermon to the first congregation to
which I was appointed in 1972. I have written down—no,
actually, I have hunted and two-finger pecked on a circa
1735 typewriter each and every word I can think of that
has anything to do with love. So far, we will be singing
the closing hymn at 11:15 a.m. Maybe they will love me
for this early out. Hmmmmmm.

I decided to go stand in the yard and lean on the
lawnmower that has been provided for us. As I leaned
and fretted a bit, I heard an old tractor coming from the
large farm adjacent to the fenced-in property on which
the parsonage sat. First, a hat came into view. Then a body

began to appear. It was a man driving a vintage John Deere. There is such a sweet sound to that tractor.

He pulled up to the fence and killed the engine. "You must be the new preacher," he said. I would be hearing that phrase again soon. And more than once.

"I am Pettus," he told me. "My wife is Lena. We are your neighbors. We live over there on the farm." He nodded to indicate a wonderful farmhouse sitting in front of a barn and several outbuildings. They also had a huge garden that covered at least half an acre. The rows were bright with vegetables, and multicolored Marigolds separated the rows and kept the bugs to a minimum.

He continued. "Our garden is coming in real good. We will keep you supplied with fresh vegetables, if that is all right."

All right, I thought, *wonderful!*

There was more.

"You see that dog pen out behind the barn? There is a brace of pointers there. As long as you are my pastor, those are your dogs. I will show you at least a dozen coveys of quail within about a half hour of the house."

And there was even more.

"You see that pond away from the house and toward your place here? It has a stream that runs through it, so it is stocked with channel catfish. As long as you are my pastor, that pond and those fish are yours. Now, one thing."

I was ready for a huge boot to drop on both my feet.

"You see that big pine on the edge of the pond?" he asked.

I nodded and waited.

"My pet albino catfish live around the roots of that tree. If you catch one, you gotta throw it back. I never keep those."

So far, not so good; so far, incredible! Wonderful! Was I in heaven or what?

Pettus was true to every word that he had spoken. And Lena was the perfect match for him. Sometimes grace comes to call to the sound of an old tractor.

There is more.

He said, "You preaching Sunday?"

Since I was the newly appointed preaching pastor, I knew the answer to that one.

"Yes, sir."

"What you gonna use as your text?"

"I am preaching on love and will use John 3:16 as the text."

Pettus thought on that a bit. Then he said, "Do you know why country folks like us can love each other so well?"

In that simple question, I knew I now had at least ten more minutes, maybe fifteen additional minutes, to that sermon I was still fretting over and not yet getting.

"No, sir, I don't know that," I told him.

I once served on a team with a bunch of men who were asked to take notes when someone spoke on a topic related to their growing in faith and in works. With the Lord as my witness, my hand is in the air that this is true. One man finally spoke as to his neglecting to write down anything.

"I was going to take some mental notes, but I didn't have anything to write on," he said.

Well, I had my mental notes ready for the outpouring of wisdom that Pettus was going to deliver my way. Praise God, my sermon would be saved!

"We love so well because we don't live close," he said. Then he cranked the tractor and drove home.

I kept leaning on the lawnmower and praying for my first sermon.

32

GNAWING LOCUSTS!

"I will restore to you the years which the swarming locust has eaten …"

—*Joel 2:25 (RSV)*

YOU ALWAYS WANT TO HANG WITH YOUR BIG BROTHER. YOU probably could, except he has "running buddies" of his own, and few—if any—of them want a younger sibling getting in the way. It has been that way for generations. My brother and I were no exception.

The night of all nights is Halloween. Though you are almost too old to "trick or treat," the candy is good. So, you borrow an old pillowcase and try to slouch a few years off your age as you go from door to door, asking for the goodies. Meanwhile, your brother's older bunch is off in a car, pranking some pranks. These included tossing lighted firecrackers in the general direction of clusters of children who are out on the sidewalks of the town.

No one ever intends for something seemingly harmless to go so wrong, but it does. In this case, one of the small children tries to pick up a dud firecracker that just sits on the ground, but it explodes.

From that night forward, you will wear a label that you did not earn. You will be forever "the guy in the car with John Gregory who hurt the little girl with the fireworks." There will be no trial. No evidence will be gathered. No eyewitness testimonies will be taken. You will move away to another area of the state, but still the legend of your supposed misdeed lingers. You will even return years later for an event in the town, and the first greeting you receive is, "You remember that night with John Gregory?"

No, you do not. But it doesn't matter. You are powerless to do anything with it. It just lingers in the air of that town.

Methodist youth camps have always been among the finest experiences that an older child or youth can be given. I was privileged for several years to serve as the TIR, or "theologian in residence," at a camp north of where we lived. The title means you preach in chapel services and hang out with the campers whenever you can.

Lord knows I love to tell stories, and captive teens can be a good audience. But the best part of those years at that youth camp were the occasions when the campers from Gracewood joined the others for events and activities and worship. These are campers with different developmental needs who add great joy and delight to everyone.

Gracewood was the most amazing ministry I have ever witnessed. Each camper from Gracewood is teamed with a college-age student who is their 24/7 buddy for the week. By the end of that time in camp, it is impossible to tell who has given and who has received the most love and grace and mercy.

One other group at camp are the pioneer campers, who live in tents, cook their own food, and generally avoid water for the entire week. One year, the camp director came to me and asked if I would travel out to the pioneer camp and lead worship that would include holy communion.

"Yes, I would be honored," I said.

When we arrived, I found that the Gracewood bunch would also be joining us for the evening's activities. We started with volleyball, and I was teamed with a young man named Jack. He was a camper at Gracewood for the first time. He was having a ball. He became my personal cheerleader.

My good shots and blocks were rewarded with, "David, that was so good."

The more frequent and not-so-good shots were greeted with, "You'll get it, David!"

As supper preparation was being assaulted by the pioneer group, some of the Gracewood buddies and campers joined me for a walk down near the small lake.

From way back in my youth and childhood, I had heard the Bobwhite Quail calling to gather the covey for the evening. My dad had taught me the simple whistle that is intended to invite the birds to call back and even to move toward you if you are convincing. That summer night, I became the "quail whistler" as several of the birds were drawn to the water for a last drink at the lake before bedtime. But to the campers, it was my whistle that brought them close.

Jack was especially appreciative and called out, "David, that is amazing."

I was red-faced, but I loved that exchange with him.

Dinner was ready. Well, the food had been sort of organized, and who doesn't like some pine straw with chicken and rice? At least the red fruit punch was almost cold. But fellowship and laughter ruled the evening. We chortled all the way until time for worship.

The pioneer group had burned the communion bread beyond recognition, but we found a partial loaf of raisin bread that was caught by its wrapper in a nearby shrubbery.

My meditation for worship was based on Jesus's words about loving one another. My illustration was to speak of the Gracewood "buddies" who I had seen giving and receiving love in exactly the way Jesus meant. I broke the raisin bread and poured fruit punch into a chalice I had brought.

After I offered the words of institution for the Lord's Supper, I asked two of the "buddies" and two of the Gracewood campers to serve the rest of us.

As I found my seat next to Jack, he reached over and patted my hand. He said, "David, you are such a good preacher."

If you have ever been around a campfire the smoke will find your eyes and cause a tear or two to drop in the night. It happened. Later, we packed up, returned to the main area, and made our way to bed on this last night of the week's camp.

Before leaving for home the next day, all the campers and staff filled up the gym, where anxious parents have also gathered. One of the perks of being TIR is that your family, including any eligible children, can attend while you serve. My wife, Billie, was also there for the week.

All the campers and staff were seated in a huge circle in the middle of the building. I saw Jack with his mob, and we waved a few at each other. During this time, official goodbyes are spoken, and then a marvelous song about "praying for you" is sung by everyone.

Our own children were already packed and ready to go after about half an hour of their own goodbyes. Our family law meant that a mandatory stop for burgers and fries was next on the agenda—just as soon as I was finished with my own farewells.

I was almost through the doors on the way to our car when a man spoke to me.

"Hello, David."

"Hi."

"This has been a great week."

"I know. We have had a ball."

I was fully edging toward my family's faces pressed against the car windows.

"And you made a preacher."

"Yeah, I did."

"My son was so blessed to be with you. I just wanted you to know. Goodbye and God bless you."

"Thank you," I said as I edged further away from him.

It was then that the man's elbow moved to one side, and Jack's face was framed between that elbow and his father's side.

I said, "Hey, Jack! See you later."

At that, the man removed a business card from his pocket and handed it to me. I pocketed the card. Then he and his son walked to their own car and drove away.

I stood watching them for a moment. Then I took out the card, turned it right-side up, and read:

John Gregory
Regional Manager
Norvell Products
3452 Industrial Way
Carrolton, GA 30112

33

EYES TO SEE

"The people walking in darkness have seen a great light ..."

—*Isaiah 9:2 (Christian Standard Bible)*

I JUST FOUND OUT HOW TO SPELL HIS NAME. IN THE LONG-gone ads, he said it was Tom Bodett. His catchphrase: "And we will leave the light on for you."

He borrowed that saying. He borrowed it from my mother, Carolyn Judith Norton Bowen, of Athens, Georgia, now a resident of heavenly places. I know he borrowed it because she had been saying those words to her children for years, long before Tom or anybody else made it famous with a TV ad.

For my life, having the light left on for you meant I was home. The light signified home. The "light left on" included dark nights after hunting or fishing all day with my dad. The "light left on" meant long bus rides after ball games. The "light left on" encompassed all those dirty-laundry trips from college, as well as those very rare flights home from the army.

Sometimes the light was on in the sleet and almost-snow of Georgia's winters. Sometimes the light was on during the storms of uncertainty and doubt and pain and loss and fear. Sometimes the light was on when there was joy and hope and peace and love and celebration and blessing.

The light was always left on for me. Having the light on meant my return home was expected. My return home was wanted. My return home was desired.

It was not a casual thing, this light. I mattered. And the light left on made that pronouncement loud and clear.

Did you read the Bible verse from Isaiah at the beginning of this section? It is timeless, and it always speaks to my heart.

Mom, thank you for all the years in which you have been a wonderful part of the light in my darkness. I love you.

You son,

David George

34

MACON IN AUGUST!

"Blessed be the LORD God of Israel, from everlasting to everlasting. Amen and amen."
—*Psalm 41:13 (Christian Standard Bible)*

HOW DEEP CAN THE CHURCH VAN TIRES SINK IN THE MOLTEN asphalt of the Shell service station just off the expressway in Macon, Georgia? Up to the rim is the answer.

If Macon did not invent summer heat, then it cosponsored the bill that made it law in August. But worse than the heat was the choice of Georgia Methodists to hold pastors' school during that scorching time. And in case something was missed, the lodging for that event was in the un-air-conditioned dorms of Mercer University.

By the way, in Georgia summers, *fan* is a noun and not a verb related to air being stirred. Yet, nevertheless, moreover, however, there were two places of relief and mercy during the three-and-one-half days of meeting: One was the cafeteria. But we were forbidden to live or even to sleep in that space. The other was the auditorium.

Spine-wrenching theater seats were staggered from the back of the building all the way down to a huge stage.

Forget about that. The place was kept pork-hanging cold.

The schedule always had at least two lecturers from way out of town. These were academic types whose books we had read or had meant to read. I still have a collection of such books from dozens of pastors' schools. But then there was the preacher for the school, from Fred Craddock to Oral Roberts—or would that be the other way round? Great sermons were delivered daily.

These were the kind of sermons that were rumored to have been revised, disguised, and reprised as if those hearing them in Macon had written them all by their lonesome.

Did I mention the singing? Lord, have mercy, such singing! We were led in the thundering hymns of the Christian faith by as skilled and polished a group of song leaders as any great crusade would have presented. In these times, sleepy eyes were awakened. Naps were interrupted. Heads popped up at the opening notes. We wanted to sing. We were led to sing. We could sing. Even if we couldn't all find the right notes, we made such a joyful noise that I believe a fragrant offering was graciously received by the Almighty.

Then came the morning/evening prayers. It was too hot during the rest of the day for anything but mild to moderate complaining. Please imagine that the Mercer Auditorium was filled to the brim with pastors and preachers and ministers from around Georgia. We had declared a truce between northern and southern Georgia so that any and all were welcome to pastors' school.

Among all these clergy were vast numbers who fiercely hoped that they would be selected to pray one of the two major prayers of the day. It was going to be the pastor from First Church in downtown there. Or the pastors who we were forbidden to know was the next district superintendent of the Here District. Occasionally, we were even led in those prayers by one chosen to become bishop at the next regional conference where clergy became bishops but never saw the honor coming.

My all-time favorite was the year the "person to pray" selection train went off the rails not so very far from the Otis Redding Memorial Bridge. All the cards got misdealt. All the arrangements got disarranged. All the plans to honor the famous or soon-to-be famed got unplanned.

His name remains a great mystery. No one then or since would take the responsibility or the blame for how he got chosen. He was a pastor. He did serve a congregation. The clergy from southern Georgia assumed he was assigned to a three- or four-point circuit north of Atlanta.

The clergy from northern Georgia figured he was serving a rural appointment in the region of Hahira. He came to the podium with spirit blazing. His voice called to mind those angelic deliveries to the likes of Josephs and Marys and wise shepherds. He laid out such an appeal to God that the pages of the books of worship in the Cokesbury sales area had a greenish tint.

We were lifted to the heights of praise and worship. We were plunged into the abyss of our low-down selfish and sinful ways. Every ear strained, and a lot of brains worked because he had to be a plant. He had to be a guest of somebody famous from outside Georgia.

Who cares? His every word fitted perfectly into its place in the prayer. "In the name of Jesus" pulled every one of us onto the closing word. We knew those words. We had heard those words. We used those words on a regular basis. In the heat of Macon, Georgia, it was not going to matter whether it was pronounced *ah-men* or *a-men*. But instead, he closed with *ar-men*.

It remains my favorite word to remind myself that far too much religion was created by us in our own image. And also to remind myself of the laughter of God.

35

WHAT CAN YOU DO?

"If you give encouraging guidance, be careful
that you don't get bossy …"

—*Romans 12:8 (The Message)*

How far did Abram travel from Ur to Haran to
Canaan? A ways. In a lot of ways.

My journey was only from Winder to Canada to
Chamblee, but it was still a ways. In a lot of ways. Back then,
Chamblee was not a part of Atlanta. In fact, I had to tell
some people that I was from Atlanta, because explaining the
location of Chamblee would have taxed their imaginations
beyond breaking.

Chamblee had its own plaza before Lennox was more
than two stores separated by long distances of imagination
and pavement. It had:

- a high school in which everybody knew your
  name.

- a transportation hub at the Oglethorpe Hill Funeral Home from which you could catch a number twenty-three Oglethorpe bus ride to Atlanta.
- a drive-in movie with seating out in front of the refreshment stand.

In those days of the early 1960s, my favorite thing about Chamblee was the people: Friends. Youth counselors at church. Teachers. Teammates on the athletic teams. Scouting buddies.

Looking back, Louis Grizzard could have written about the characters in Chamblee. He would have been just as accurate in describing the people as he was about Moreland, Georgia, where he lived.

What in the world do you remember about those years before you got to be nineteen or twenty? Far too much to recall. Some of it is best forgotten. I do remember the women who prayed for us, especially when we did not know we were covered with a loving blanket of grace.

High school is necessary for life. But being there dictates that you will be so self-conscious that you fail to see how much love is spoken on your behalf as praying.

One of those women who prayed for me was Doris Brown. We lost her to death at age 99.5. She was an encourager in the best sense of that word. Look it up. Far too often in our Puritan-tinged religious heritage, the word meant *exhorter*. Look that one up.

I have had exhorters in my life. I had them back then. An example of exhortation would be when you made a ninety-seven on a major assignment. The person who exhorts you would ask, "Did they give any one hundreds?"

You already knew the answer, so why that kind of question? It was to shove you into doing closer to perfection. Was the question helpful? Useful? Realistic for you?

I thought of Doris. I am so thankful to God that she purposefully lived out the spiritual gift of "encouraging."

May I tell you how she encouraged me? I have always loved words. I have always written words in my mind and sometimes on paper. However, I kept my words a secret for a long time.

Once, I offered a few of my written words in the form of poems to a Chamblee High School publication. They were as awkward as I was.

Most people who commented said nice things. Those comments are always appreciated.

You know what Doris Brown said to me? "David, you need to write. I hope you will."

How did she know that one of the deepest longings of my heart was to put my words on paper and also to share them with others? How could she know that I needed to write when I was the only person who did?

Because she was given the gift of encouraging others. Thank you, Doris!

36

LIGHT AS A FEATHER

"For everything there is a season, and a time for every matter under heaven …"

—*Ecclesiastes 3:1 (English Standard Version)*

WHAT DO THE FIRST EIGHT VERSES IN ECCLESIASTES 3, THE Canon in D by Johann Pachelbel, and the movie *Forrest Gump* have in common? They are all part of a story. May I tell that story this morning?

He left a diary. He left a journal on whose pages are written some of the details of his life's journey. The words are written on a small, college-ruled, black and white notebook like this. He grew up in a home where Bible verses were important, but most often, it was just the verses. Not much was said or asked about the context or about where the verses were located in the larger story of God and Jesus and the Holy Spirit. Yet, he had always been drawn to the words from Ecclesiastes 3. Do you know them?

He practiced poetry in private. No, he practiced reading and writing poetry in secret. Athletics? Very much publicly, yes. Scouting, hiking, and canoeing and camping around the Charles L. Summers Canoe Base outside Ely, Minnesota, and Rainy Mountain near Clayton, Georgia. More publicly, yes.

He was also drawn to music. In private. His first round, plastic-grooved disc thing was by Buddy Holly out of Lubbock, Texas. His second was *Messiah* by Handel. Close behind were other so-called classical pieces like Symphony no. 3 by Saint-Saens. And then Jimmy Jones with *Good Timin'*. Who could ever forget:

> *If little David hadn't grabbed that stone*
> *Lyin' there on the ground*
> *Big Goliath might've stomped on him*
> *Instead of the other way round*
> *But he had*
> *Timin' a tick a tick a tick a*
> *Good timin' a tock a tock a tock a tock a*
> *Timin' is the thing it's true*
> *Good timin' brought me to you*

But especially the Canon in D by Pachelbel. A canon is a polyphonic device in which several voices play the same music, entering in sequence.

For this man, it really did seem that there were seasons and times when things in life were so different and so opposite of what they had just been. As you grow, there come other seasons of blessing and loss into your life. Like a night in May where you learn that your marriage is way past over. What you had thought were plans for your future are no more.

But May is only a short season. Then comes June.

He boarded a transatlantic jet to spend the summer in another country with the two children for whom he was now sole custodial parent.

Have you ever been in a time or in a place where there is nothing you can do? What did you do? Isn't that the truth? You reach a place and a time when you can do nothing. So, what do you do?

He remembered the wall of pain that is a gift of most sports. In fact, the wall of pain or the wall of your limits is available in a lot of life's phases.

For him, that wall was always in the background as he ran. Why not run now that your marriage is gone, your children are totally yours, and your support system is so far away? Why not run?

Shoes can be purchased throughout the world. So can lightweight June, July, and August running gear.

Do you run? Have you run? What is in your head while you run?

For this man, now running through the almost completely empty streets of a small town in England, it was music that came into his head. He tried rock and roll—Little Richard and the Allman Brothers. He tried psychedelic, Jefferson Airplane. He tried country, Dolly and Hank. He even tried all old hymns, but none of that music was quite right.

The music that was in his head was softer and without a driving beat to which you might judge a nine on the Dick

Clark American Bandstand. It was this piece of classical music called Canon in D by Pachelbel.

But even that was not enough. Now there were words behind and around and beneath this music that were filling up his brain.

He would not want me to tell you this. He was not well. In fact, he was so unwell that the words from Ecclesiastes 3 begin to fit themselves to the Canon in D. How?

Ecclesiastes 3:1–8 is a poem. It may not rhyme, but it is a poem, and when poems are set to music, you get a song. A hymn.

It must have been a sight for the residents of the small town as the man ran with headphones on while singing Ecclesiastes 3 to a tune by Pachelbel. He ran until he found the wall of pain. Then he ran beside that wall until he ran through it.

The idea he told me was this: The physical pain moved all of the emotional and heart and soul pain to another place. And this, dear friend, is where Forrest Gump enters the story.

Do you recall his running? Not the Alabama touchdown runs or the run to save Bubba's life as he bled to death in Forrest's arms. Until what day did Forrest run? He ran until he did not need to run anymore.

It seems there is a season and a time for everything, including a time to run and a time to go home. He left for home to get his children back in school for the fall, yet the words of Ecclesiastes never left him.

May I read from his journal?

"There are seasons of our lives that are given as part of

our being created by God. We are not in charge of these seasons and time. We are not in control of these times and seasons."

When you read the twenty-eight "times" in Ecclesiastes, do you recognize that they are part of every life?

So much for Ecclesiastes 3:1–8. The writer of Ecclesiastes introduced us to a word that we misunderstand about as much as any other word in human language. The word is *hebel* in Hebrew. The usual translation is "vanity or useless or meaningless." A better translation is "vaporous" or "like fog or a light mist." You cannot catch it or hold it in your hand. You cannot own or control or manipulate it. To sum up the rest of the Ecclesiastes in simple English:

- Nothing we own,
- Nothing we have,
- Nothing we do,
- Nothing we make,
- Nothing we learn,
- Nothing we know,
- Nothing we build, and
- Nothing we can figure out is ultimately satisfying.

We can use all that stuff for an idol to worship. We can use all that stuff and more for an addiction. But it is never, never ultimately satisfying.

How then shall we live? In light of Ecclesiastes 3:1–8, how shall we live? Treasure family. Treasure friends.

Treasure good food that you do not have to show off to enjoy. Treasure frequent laughter.

Thank God for these everyday gifts in your life.

The man I spoke about still does. You already know his name, don't you? That's right.

David G. Bowen.

37

A FRIEND FOR LIFE

"And the two good-for-nothing persons came
in and took their seats ..."

—*1 Kings 21:13 (Bible in Basic English)*

DID YOU EVER HAVE AN IMAGINARY FRIEND IN YOUR LIFE? I
did. His name was Jim. He was probably a character in
one of the dozens of books that I munched on like caramel
popcorn at our library, but it didn't matter. He was my best
friend.

Like Puff and other magical beings, Jim began to fade
and leave my imagination as I approached the stage of
denial that is required to "grow up." I missed him.

Then one day, it happened. I was assigned as pastor to
a church in a small town.

Is it "hey day" or "hay day" that a congregation
remembers when most of the young people leave for other
places? Either way, it hurts.

One way to deny the hurt and loss is to become rigid
with the standards of who is welcome in the activities of the

church. For instance, we had a family with small children who moved to the town. They brought themselves and their four children to Sunday school and to worship. This family contacted me about joining the church. I said yes. How about the next Sunday?

That day came. I was at my invitational best as the closing hymn was announced. The adults agreed to the words of transferring membership and pledged to support the ministries of the congregation. They were smiling. I was grinning. I was grinning so hard that I failed to notice some of the nods and frowns on the faces of a group of church members.

Not everyone, but enough.

It was home and lunch and the sofa for me after morning worship. Then came the knock at the front door. As I opened the door, I was greeted by the collected faces of the group. They asked if we could talk.

Our conversation was "unofficial," of course. They just wanted me to know that some people who attended our church might not really be comfortable with joining and becoming members.

What was I to do?

"Well, why don't you contact some of us when you have someone who might want to join? That way, we can meet with them and discover whether or not they will be comfortable enough to join us," I suggested.

May I tell you what I heard them say?

The family that joined was Sears-and-Roebuck-catalogue people in the way they spoke and dressed and acted. I was supposed to cultivate only the people who were

Rich and Macy's in the way they lived and moved and had what the others had.

You know that things just feel wrong even though everyone else says it is right? That was how I felt—mostly confused and very saddened.

Just about then, Jim and his family began attending. He was a professional, a small-business owner. He and his wife were both college graduates. And then some. I figured they would be acceptable.

Jim stopped me at the sanctuary on their first Sunday to ask if I was a dove hunter. He owned a farm outside of town and was going to plant a field of brown-top millet. He wondered if I wanted to help with the planting, and then I would be welcome to shoot over that field as well.

He did not stop there.

He'd heard I was a duck hunter and asked if I would be interested in shooting some ducks when the season arrived later that year. I both thought about and said yes to Jim's invitation in about two-hundred ways that day.

I also thought to myself that the very unofficial "committee" that had come to see me could kiss my grits. But Sunday came.

I noticed that Jim, his wife, and their two children had arrived a few minutes early for worship that morning. They had chosen to sit in a pew about four from the back of the sanctuary and had settled in.

I was taking care of preacher things up near the pulpit when I noticed that most of the congregation was looking back to where Jim and his family were seated. Standing in the aisle was a couple who were both fervently praying that the glory days of the church would return and that no stranger would be allowed to sit in "their" pew.

I have since worshipped in Virginia and other locations where a family does actually own the "box" in which their pew is located. They pay money to ensure that such an embarrassing debacle that occurred because of Jim and his family would never happen to them.

I guess Jim did not know the rules of pew ownership, and thus, he did not notice the couple standing in the aisle just out of his peripheral vision. It seemed like hours with the tension building up like the closing aria of some opera.

Finally, enough "ahems" and coughs and shuffling had been done so that Jim looked up with a puzzled look on his face.

"You are in our pew," the couple said with about as much cold as homemade peach ice cream requires.

Apologies and "excuse us" were both offered. But then it became clear that the offended couple owned the entire pew and not just the two seats that Jim offered by moving his family down the pew by at least two adult spaces.

Finally, the continuing-to-be-wounded man and woman were able to reclaim their stolen seats and peace settled over the church.

To their credit, Jim and his family joined the congregation with the approval of all who spoke to me. They remained faithful members who lived out their pledge to pray and attend and give and serve. Our friendship grew, and we shared about as deep a friendship as was possible.

Unfortunately, preachers get transferred, and so it was with me. Time and distance and real life often make it impossible to continue relationships, even the strongest ties that we could wish to have.

Years passed. Then one day, I was contacted by Jim's family to see if I would return to do his funeral. Of course I would. The service was to be in the funeral home and his burial in the town cemetery.

I was blessed to see several old friends from my days as pastor in that place. I chose to base my remarks on Romans 8. I also used the words of Robert Louis Stevenson in "Requiem": "Home is the sailor, home from sea, and the hunter home from the hill."

The drive to the cemetery was too somber for the joy that I had experienced in Jim's friendship. The walk to the grave was silent. But I know that grief and death make most of us very uncomfortable. We just do not know how to act with the reality of either of those things.

I could see the funeral home tent rising ahead of where we were walking. As we approached, I stepped to my place inside the low granite walls, and something caught my eye. I could see that Jim was being buried next to a gravesite where two headstones declared that a couple was already interred.

Of course, that couple were the same two people who had stood in the sanctuary aisle so that Jim and his family would be uncomfortable enough to move from their personal pew. I don't know what is officially acceptable as far as guffawing or laughter or giggling at gravesides in the South. If there are rules on such, I totally broke all of them that day.

Rest well, my friend.

38

CONNECTING THE DOGS

"Oh, taste and see that the Lord is good ..."
—*Psalm 34:8 (English Standard Version)*

REMEMBER WHEN THE ATHENS, GEORGIA, VARSITY Restaurant was right downtown? I do. A group of us went there on lots of Friday nights in cold weather. We would travel from Winder to Stegmann Hall at the University of Georgia to several hours of "open pool" swimming with whoever else showed up. It was cool to imagine we were college students just hanging around the pool.

I think it cost a whole dollar for the privilege. But that was just the beginning of the cool evening. The next step was a gastronomic delight for anyone who knew hot dogs were a gift like ambrosia in a bun. Add chili, mustard, and lots of smushed onions, and maybe even slaw if you are older.

"What'll ya have?"

Exactly. Fries or rings, and who would want to deny a peach pie?

We would stay as long as the chauffeuring adult would tolerate. We basked in the smells and sounds and sights of what we wanted to do when we finally got to grow up.

Some people don't get to stay in Winder forever. I was travelling to Canada to the Boundary Waters north of Ely, Minnesota, when my family moved to Chamblee, Georgia, in June. That meant new everything on the face of the earth: new house, school, sports teams, church, faces, imaginations. You name it, and it changed to something new.

Then Rem and John stepped up. "We are going to Atlanta for food and a movie. Wanna go?" they asked me.

You already got some of this. We went downtown to the original home of the fabulously delightful hot dog, the Varsity on North Avenue. I had never seen a carhop or anything quite like the long lines that were at least half-filled with insomniac Georgia Tech students.

But "What'll ya have" rang out, and I was saved.

How do I describe the Fox Theatre? If you know, you understand. Small town, come to real town!

Thank you, John and Rem. It mattered.

Please step into the "way-forward" machine, not the "way-back." Dial-in Cobb County, Georgia, and make it some thirty-one years later. The congregation I was serving was smack in the middle of the third fastest-growing census tract in sight. There were new members on most Sundays. There were lots of professions of faith and baptism. Weddings happened all over the place.

Many families came from places north of Virginia with numerous consonants in the state names. They showed up and kept coming. One couple had four children and were very supportive of what we were doing in the community and how we were doing it.

Of course, in sermons, I would regularly mention the Varsity, as required by liturgical protocol.

Then, a family quit appearing. I ran into the mother one evening in Kroger. It was near the canned vegetables. She saw me, but it was too late for her to duck away with style.

I said that we had missed them in worship. She acknowledged that they were attending another congregation.

We both paused. Then she said, "Do you know why?"

I had no idea.

"We were planning a huge family event with folks coming from out of town, and we wondered about a place to dine. You had made such a fuss about this exclusive downtown Atlanta dinner club that we all decided to meet there."

She paused to gather her formidable indignation. Then she said, "David, it is a hot dog joint. It is not even a restaurant!"

Obviously, I was not going to let this slide as it perhaps deserved.

"Yes," I said, "And I hope you got the rings and a peach pie!"

39

THE NEWBIE IS ALWAYS SENT!

"Naked I came from my mother's womb, and
naked I will depart. The LORD gave and the
LORD has taken away; may the name of the
LORD be praised."

—*Job 1:21 (New International Version)*

THE PHONE CALL CAME ABOUT THREE AND A HALF WEEKS
after I moved to the small town in Georgia. I was the newly
appointed pastor in charge of the First United Methodist
Church. The caller identified himself as one of the owners
of the local funeral home. He welcomed me to town. Then
he asked if I ever did a funeral service for someone not in
my congregation.

I could sense my false pride and self-righteousness
moving to my voice box. "Of course," I said, trying to
sound just as much like a nonjudgmental follower of Jesus
as I could.

"Good. There has been a death. The rest of the family

lives out of town. They have no church affiliation and are looking for a pastor willing to bury their father."

He gave me the address of the deceased and told me that the man's three daughters would be at that house after three o'clock that afternoon. I set my mental times. I checked my GPS stuff for the address and for the directions to get there.

Everything was good to go. I would be making a name for myself in that community. Humble disciple, who cares? Sounds about right.

What could be better? What could possibly go wrong? I pulled out of the church parking lot and headed up the four-lane to the left turn that was several miles out of town. It was then that I noticed the sign announcing what was located at the end of the road on which I was travelling.

It was a nudist colony!

Say what?

I said several prayers that I had never uttered before as I drove up to the welcome booth. I got directions to the right house and drove away with more questions than I had answers. The one that loomed significantly was: "Three daughters with whom I am to meet and plan this funeral."

Three daughters.

The cry of my heart was answered as one of the women opened the front door in response to my ringing the bell. She must have read my mind as well as my puzzled face.

"You are probably wondering about us and nudist camps," she said. "We quit that when we left home to begin our own lives. None of us has gone back."

Thank you, God! I thought. I began to breathe for the

first time since I had pulled my car into the area of the welcome booth.

The daughters were gracious and very helpful. I was told that their father had weighed over three-hundred pounds at his death. We never covered this in my pastoral counseling courses at Emory. What would Joe Whitwell do? What did Wayne Oates cover in that chapter on funerals?

His daughters offered more gracious help. "We are having him cremated," they said.

Thank you, God! I thought.

Thus, began a most excellent conversation about the man's life and how they wanted to celebrate him. We would be holding the funeral service in the chapel of the funeral home. The music would be provided by a local musician. I would be speaking. Others would be invited to share a memory of the man after my words were finished. I asked the daughters to describe their father's life and to share with me any stories that we could use to honor him.

He had a great spirit of being a neighbor. If anyone was sick or hurt, he was the first to offer help. After any sickness or death, he was the first to arrive with casseroles and words of sympathy. If someone struggled to pay a utility bill because of economic hardship, he paid it as anonymously as possible.

As the daughters talked, an image of this man began to form in my mind. He simply knew about and further lived out the basics of being a great neighbor. The image continued. He lived with just the basic necessities of life.

Still further did the image go, until I busted out laughing.

Three heads turned and three sets of eyes focused on my attempt to be cool.

"What is it?" they asked.

I prayed. Then I told them the truth. In my mind, the image of their beloved father was that of Baloo the Bear in *The Jungle Book* by Kipling.

You begin to see it, yes? The song is "Bare Necessities."

I took a deep breath and continued. "I would like to read some of the lyrics of that song as part of your dad's service. Is that possible? I would not wish to offend you or anyone by the humor, but the song speaks to his heart and to his spirit of mercy."

There was a pause. Thoughts were thought. Ideas came and went. Finally, they agreed. And so it was that on a bright afternoon in the funeral home of a small Georgia town, a crowd gathered, and the preacher read from "Bare Necessities" as part of his eulogy. After the service, I spoke to the daughters and offered to arrange a service for the interment of their father's ashes if and when that was appropriate. The eldest asked if I was coming back to the house for refreshments. If so, we could talk there. I was, and we did.

After a time of greeting and some brief remarks of thanks by the daughters, we met outside the front door.

"We are going to keep Dad with Mom. At least for a while," they said.

That same look of *say what?* crossed my face. After a pause for laughter, they led me to the side yard. There was a tree whose lower limbs had been shaped and formed into something like a small platform.

On that platform was an urn that contained Mom. Or, at least, her ashes. With a great sweep of grace, the youngest daughter placed Dad beside Mom. This part of the journey was finished.

"We also have colored spotlights so they can be seen at night," she said.

It turns out that, in that town, the latest hired employee of utility companies, vending companies, and even newly appointed pastors are sent out to the nudist colony as a way to welcome them to the neighborhood.

It was, in fact, an honor for me.

40

WON'T YA LET ME TAKE YOU ON A SEA CRUISE!

"O taste and see that the Lord is good ..."
—*Psalm 34:8 (King James Version)*

EVER SINCE I CAN REMEMBER, MY FATHER WANTED TO LIVE in Alaska. He never did. In fact, he never even got to visit there, but I did. This telling of a story is dedicated to him. Love ya, Bill.

My wife, Billie, and I were excited to join family and friends for a cruise up the Inside Passage and then spend another week exploring the land of that magnificent state. I had been on several cruises before. These included the Okefenokee Swamp, Lake Lanier, and the Boundary Waters north of Ely, Minnesota, but nothing even came close to joining several thousand passengers and crew on a ship larger than my vivid imagination.

We left the harbor of Seattle, Washington, and off we sailed through some of the most eye-stretching and heart-enhancing country I have ever seen. We had already signed up for several excursions, or side trips, to places and sights that the eleven-color brochure insisted had to be seen. I knew my favorite was going to be whale watching.

Our ship dropped anchor in a huge expanse of water, and we took a launch to a dock connected to the shore. We were to enjoy waiting there and, what a surprise, shopping opportunities, while the first group of Leviathan watchers had their time with the humpbacks.

Now, I am not a person of competition. But when I saw a huge board on which the different whale-watching groups reported all the beasts and creatures they saw during their excursions, my heart leapt because I knew in that moment that our group would see at least one more of something than any of the others.

Billie and I were joined by my favorite sister, Judy, from Virginia. When people ask me about her, I always say, "Not quite as tall as me. More hair. Strange sense of humor. Very intelligent." She is also great fun to hang with, and this trip to Alaska was a total treat for me since we don't live close to each other.

Finally, it was time. The first group came into the harbor and began to unload. They sent a two-people delegation to write their sightings on the board. My heart was stuck in my throat as they wrote the numbers:

- 3 humpbacks.
- 2 orcas.
- 1 otter or seal, not sure.

Alas. Alack. Woe will be our group if this warm-up bunch had that kind of miserable luck.

Billie and Judy and I moved down the dock and gangway and onto a boat about the size of one of Captain Anderson's deep-sea fishing boats out of Panama City, Florida. There were just enough people on board with us to fill a third of the capacity. I thought, *Word must have gotten out that the sea life is hiding today so people would rather shop.*

We shoved off and out into the icy straits of Alaska. The three of us found a long bench below the main deck so we were out of the swirling winds and trying to talk like it didn't matter what we saw or didn't see.

Suddenly, there was a yell. "Breach!" someone said.

If you have ever been on one of these boats, when the crowd all rushes to one side, you can tell. We threw down our excess stuff and rushed topside to see humpback after humpback fully stretching out of the water and into the air.

There were some whales so close that we believed we could touch them. Full adults and several babies, if you can call something that is twenty feet long and that weighs more than four cars a baby.

This went on for days. Actually, we saw whales all over the place for as long as the excursion lasted. I was hoping for a three-hour tour, but we only got about two hours of whale loving. I got so excited that I forgot I was a mature adult and just yelled and screamed and pointed and shouted like every other person on that boat. Including the crew.

Finally, the hour of our departure came and we left. The excitement just kept bubbling over all of us. We made our way back to the dock. Our delegation ran like school children to write our sightings on the board.

It was almost painful that many of the passengers on that first Whale Watching Excursion had to witness as our team wrote:

- 53 humpbacks, at least because we lost count. Dozens breaching.
- No orcas.
- No otters or seals.

It was almost painful. Could it get any better?

Well, I spotted a sign that read "Crab legs available now." Judy and Billie and I never hesitated. We just bought and buttered and laughed and ate crab legs at a wooden table on a dock in a large bay in Alaska while visions of humpbacks danced in our heads.

It doesn't need to get any better!

41

I-75 ... FAR FROM CIVILIZATION

"And he disappeared from their sight."
—*Luke 24:31 (NIV)*

WHO HAS THE BEST JOKES IN YOUR COMMUNITY? I AM SURE you know, or you would not be reading this story from me. My experience is that many of the people who work in funeral homes have a sense of humor that includes great jokes and especially great stories.

John was one of those. He tells this one. He says it really happened. I believe him. He and his assistant, Jack, were travelling to way-down-south, Georgia, to pick up the body of a person who had died. They were traveling back to their funeral home in northeast Georgia.

The journey was long, and a stop for fuel and a snack were in order. As they pulled into the gas station, they both noticed a man from their own town who was thumbing a ride home on the expressway ramp.

John suggested that they offer him a ride. So after they finished their business inside the station, he told Jack to get in the back of the hearse. He did.

John started the engine and pulled the hearse over to the entrance ramp and rolled down his window.

"Hey," he spoke. "Are you going home?"

"Yes, I am," the man replied.

"Would you want to ride with me?"

"Yeah. But I am not getting in the back if you got a body."

"Well, I do. But you can hop in and ride up front with me. No problem," John said.

The man did.

They drove onto the expressway and up toward Atlanta, making small talk about life and the weather and family. The drive was going well, and they sped past a southern Georgia river swamp.

A hearse has two compartments. The cab has two seats: one for a driver and one for a passenger. It was here that John and the hitchhiking man were sitting and talking. The rest of the hearse is a space for a casket, and the two compartments are separated by a sliding-glass window.

Jack was quietly sitting in that rear compartment on a small seat like a flight attendant would occupy in flight. He had purchased cigarettes at the gas station, but he had failed to secure a light for them.

Simple. He reached forward and opened the sliding-glass window and said, "Hey John. You got a light?"

Without a word, the passenger opened the door of the hearse and disappeared into the swamp. When John tells this story, he says that as far as he and Jack could tell, the man's feet never broke the surface of the water as he ran for his life.

I believe him.

42

IT WOULD HAVE BEEN ENOUGH!

"I am giving you a new command: that you keep on loving each other. In the same way that I have loved you, you are also to keep on loving each other."

—*John 14:34 (The Complete Jewish Bible)*

THE SETTING FOR THE SCRIPTURE FROM JOHN IS THE FAREWELL address of Jesus to the twelve disciples. A portion of Jesus's words are directed to Peter as the one who would betray him.

Peter was outraged. He was pouting. Hurt. Frustrated. Anguished. Ashamed. And scared. But later, this same "rock" named Peter would come to understand that a far-greater plan for humanity was unfolding through Jesus's words and actions.

The heart of that plan is the love of God through the love of Jesus, through the love of the disciples, through the love that we have received and are giving. It would have been enough for Jesus to love those who would follow Him. I thank God that there was so much more that includes us.

It would have been enough for Carolyn to have grown up on an incredible farm at the edge of Athens, Georgia. She delighted in shapes and colors and patterns that many people cannot see. Far ahead of the "norm" for women of her day, she attended the University of Georgia and earned a degree in textile and fashion design.

Her dream was the Big Apple, New York City, where an incredible career for a young woman in the late 1930s awaited her. When she left town, the *Athens Banner Herald* headline read, "Local Girl Makes Good in the Big City!"

She was part of a Presbyterian congregation in Athens, but she still found time to serve on a committee at the nearby Princeton Methodist Church. That committee provided a proper welcome for the newly appointed pastor of that congregation. He was a ministerial student from Ashland, Alabama.

It would have been enough for Carolyn to give up her dream of New York and marry Bill. They dreamed of having children, and she became pregnant. Things went fine for a long time. There was great rejoicing in two families and in the small congregation they were serving while Bill finished his degree. But late in her pregnancy, Carolyn's kidneys began to malfunction. She came within an eyelash of death. Their child was stillborn.

It would have been enough for her to make the rest of her life as a storehouse for dreams and hopes and memories. However, she and her husband still wanted children. The advice of medical professionals was that further pregnancy for her would carry significant risks.

With her life at stake, she gave birth to Charles and seven years later, to Judy. In between those two children, Carolyn gave birth to me on April 6, 1945, her much-beloved middle child.

I have come to know that love is often risky and costly. Nevertheless, we are loved. And we love.

Happy Mother's Day, Carolyn. And to all of you whose love makes such a difference!

43

IT WAS ON TV

"Has become like a dove, silly and without common sense ..."

—*Hosea 7:11 (Common English Bible)*

WERE YOU EVER PART OF A MUSICAL OR A DRAMA OR A PLAY? For me, it was sixteen years between my first and my second experiences with such. The first was as M. Lindsay Woolsey in *Auntie Mame*, adapted by Jerome Lawrence and Robert Edwin Lee. "What a day! On our feet for five hours, no lunch. Why don't they put a bar in FAO Schwartz?" I loved me some Chamblee High School.

The second part I played was as the disciple Matthew in *Celebrate Life* by Buryl Red and Ragan Courtney. "Hello! My name is Matthew. And these are my friends and coworkers." I loved me some Wesley Chapel United Methodist Church.

Sometimes famous or nearly famous preachers continue with drama and even build a sermon or a worship experience around it.

In this story, he was not just "nearly anything." He was the real deal back in those days. He had a huge building in which the Sunday congregation would gather. Eleven o'clock worship time came, and the sanctuary was packed out for the music and the message. There were TV cameras all over the place, but particularly on him.

OK, so his hair piece was not like what a really good politician or actor might wear, but it was adequate.

Earlier that morning the deacon for that Sunday had taken the large spool of thin, flexible wire and securely fastened one end to the railing in the balcony. The spool was then tossed to one of the ushers, who was standing below on the floor of the sanctuary. That usher unrolled the wire so that it ran almost taut from the balcony railing to the altar table in the center of the elevated altar area, where the clear plexiglass pulpit was located. The theory was good and sound. Unfortunately, the wire was not privy to the plan devised by the preacher and those assisting in it.

Short version: as the wire was unrolled toward the pulpit, it twisted just enough for a tiny kink to have been born about halfway down to the altar area. Because the lighting was focused on the area soon to be occupied by the preacher, the kink went unseen and unnoticed by everyone there.

Worship began at eleven o'clock. The announcements were brief and to the point. The congregational singing could have moved the walls of the building some two and a half feet as building expansion might have been required for that volume of joyful song.

The prayers were clear and concise, and the special

music set just the right tone for the scriptures that would follow. The preacher opened his floppy-back Bible, and he read Mark 1:9–11 in the King James Version:

"And it came to pass in those days, that Jesus came from Nazareth of Galilee, and was baptized of John in Jordan. And straightway coming up out of the water, he saw the heavens opened, and the Spirit like a dove descending upon him: And there came a voice from heaven, saying, Thou art my beloved Son, in whom I am well pleased."

The Bible remained open to that passage and rested in the preacher's outstretched hands.

"Can you see it?" he asked. "Can you see how the glory of God is revealed as the heavens open like a massive curtain? Can you see how the totality of that glory begins to move from on high toward Jesus as he kneels in the water of the Jordan?"

That was the signal for which the deacon on the front row of the balcony had been waiting. He removed a life-size and accurately feathered model of a dove from a bag at his feet and attached the bird to the wire that was now running to where the preacher was waiting.

"Can you see the Spirit of God descending like a dove and resting upon Jesus?" the preacher asked.

The congregation turned almost as one head toward where the preacher pointed upward. The deacon gently pushed the dove so that it began a slow and dramatic descent on the wire toward the altar area.

The lighting was perfect. The people were spellbound. The artificial dove's feathers gleamed and glistened in the brightness of all the lights.

It was a perfect moment until the dove located the tiny kink in the wire. And just like another dove from the Book of Genesis, this dove alighted on that twist in the wire and came to rest.

"Can you see the dove coming down to light on our Lord?" the preacher asked. But the dove did not respond.

The deacon began to shake the wire as much as he dared, hoping that the bird would continue its downward flight. It did not.

The last thing I remember of that morning was the two ushers tossing a hardback hymnal upward from the floor of the sanctuary toward the dove to dislodge it.

44

JOHN

"This is the child God has graciously given your servant."

—*Genesis 33:5 (NIV, David Bowen adaptation)*

I FIRST MET HIM AT EMORY UNIVERSITY HOSPITAL. HE WAS a pair of eyes and a nose peeking out from beneath a blue, tightly wound baby blanket.

It was June 21, 1973, and I was a father. He was magnificent. He still is.

We named him *John* in honor of his mother's favorite uncle. We also named him Dylan in honor of the crossroads of two wordsmiths. One is a Welsh poet, and the other is a singer-songwriter from Hibbing, Minnesota.

From that first day, it was obvious that he was highly intelligent. One of the markers of such is ambidexterity. I soon learned that he could throw his milk in a glass bottle with either hand, and seldom would he miss a metal object of one kind or another. It was also obvious that he

167

was going to crawl and walk earlier than the chart in the pediatrician's office suggested he would.

John loved to swing and to rock and to help me relax in my Pauley's Island hammock in the backyard. He also grasped language skills at an accelerated rate.

I remember the time he was steering the car from the back seat in his certified child safety seat. In his quiet voice, he asked, "Dad, how do ants sweat?"

Fortunately, I had learned about exoskeletons in high school general science. Thus, I was able to answer him with a sentence or two about how ants get rid of excess moisture as part of their digestive systems. And now, at least one of you is going to look that up on the internet.

I also recall the time we were going past the Atlanta Airport and realized that John was tracking all three jets that were landing simultaneously on three different runways. Another wonder with him was the afternoon he found that the sun and moon were both clearly visible in the sky at the same time. This fact did a bit of damage to all my shared wisdom about how the sun was meant for daytime and the moon was meant for night.

But perhaps my most-favorite John moment was the time he answered my rhetorical question in morning worship. We were looking at the verse in the Hebrew scriptures of the Old Testament concerning "fear of the Lord."

The verse was Proverbs 19:23 (NIV). It reads: "The fear of the LORD leads to life; then one rests content, untouched by trouble."

I asked the gathered people what they thought "fear of the Lord" meant in language we could understand. It got

Methodistically quiet. Then someone announced that John was raising his hand to answer me. You never know what you are going to hear from any child who volunteers to speak in worship.

The congregation leaned forward into the hymnal racks. It got even quieter.

"John, what do you think?" I asked.

"Fear of the Lord means totally awesome respect," he replied.

Would you think about John's answer for a moment just as I did that morning and just as I have in the all the years since that morning? It was wonderful! Well played! I had never heard it better!

Thus, I stand at the threshold of John's birthday on June 21 and Father's day on June 20. I believe it is possible to honor someone and to be honored at the same time.

His name is John. He is my beloved son!